THE PATTERNS OF SOCIAL BEHAVIOR SERIES
Zick Rubin, *Brandeis University, General Editor*

This series brings both psychological and sociological perspectives to bear on the ways in which people affect one another. Each volume explores research on a particular aspect of social behavior and considers its personal and social implications.

a psychology
of building

Glenn **Robert Lym** received his B. Architecture degree at the University of California, Berkeley, and his Ph.D. in social psychology from Harvard University. He currently practices architecture in the San Francisco Bay area and is a lecturer in the department of architecture at Berkeley.

A SPECTRUM BOOK   PRENTICE-HALL, INC., Englewood Cliffs, New Jersey 07632

a psychology of building

how we shape and experience our structured spaces

glenn robert lym

Library of Congress Cataloging in Publication Data

Lym, Glenn Robert..
   A psychology of building.

   (The Patterns of social behavior series)
(A Spectrum Book)
   Includes bibliographical references and index.
   1. Space (Architecture) 2. Architecture—
Psychological aspects. I. Title.
NA2765.L95   720′.1   79–24177
ISBN 0–13–735225–5
ISBN 0–13–735217–4 pbk.

Editorial production/supervision by Heath Silberfeld
Interior design by Jeannette Jacobs and Dawn L. Stanley
Page Layout by Anne Bonanno
Cover photo and design by Peter Ross
Manufacturing buyer: Barbara A. Frick

A SPECTRUM BOOK

Printed in the United States of America

10 9 8 7 6 5 4 3 2 1

PRENTICE-HALL INTERNATIONAL, INC., *London*
PRENTICE-HALL OF AUSTRALIA PTY. LIMITED, *Sydney*
PRENTICE-HALL OF CANADA, LTD., *Toronto*
PRENTICE-HALL OF INDIA PRIVATE LIMITED, *New Delhi*
PRENTICE-HALL OF JAPAN, INC., *Tokyo*
PRENTICE-HALL OF SOUTHEAST ASIA PTE. LTD., *Singapore*
WHITEHALL BOOKS LIMITED, *Wellington, New Zealand*

For Ruth
who helped nurture the spaces
in which I wrote

contents

an overview   xvii

1 **romance with space**   1
neutral versus acute space   2
the western denial   6
chronic space   8
the intelligence of space   13

2 **spatial orders**   15
learning and thinking with space   16
symbol formation and spatial orders   25

3 **the spatial order of the home**   31
the internal order of the home   32
the external order of the home   48
taliesin   54
being our own architects   61

4 **professional building**   63
personal expression and the architect   64
the spatial orders of professional designers   68
the problematic relationship
of professional and users' spatial orders   81

building homes with strategic vision 95 **5**

political interests in design 96

the kitchen 97

the dark wood fortress 101

the small house 106

conflicting spatial orders 112

**building large institutions
with strategic vision** 155 **6**

the att offices 116

kresge college 124

marin county civic center 137

strategic vision 147

index 151

an overview

THE premise of this book is that we think about life through our experience and shaping of space. This means that conducting our lives in space is like a dream, a form of visual-spatial imagination, a form of thought.

This book begins with an analysis of our daily, moment-to-moment experience of space and notes the unity there between our lives, our impressions of space, and our impulses to shape that shape. Later, we will look at large building complexes and examine the evolution of social institutions and their impulses to shape space.

chapter one: romance with space

We begin with our infrequent experience of acute space in which we sense that the boundary between ourselves and ordinary neutral space has dissolved. Here, we merge vividly with space, and our understanding of ourselves becomes one and the same as our understanding of space. We go on to look at our experience of chronic space in our daily lives and its attendant space rituals.

chapter two: spatial orders

We explore the social and psychological mechanisms at work in acute and chronic space experience, turning our attention to an important product of that experience. From our experiences of space, we formulate spatial standards by which to shape and select environments for ourselves. These standards are our spatial orders.

chapter three: the spatial order of the home

We explore how we act as our architects as we go through life making homes. We follow the lives of a number of famous and not so famous individuals and observe how they evolve personal spatial orders of home in the process of finding, building, and destroying their housing.

chapter four: professional building

Here we look directly at architecture and find that professional designers do what lay people do when they see space and build. Namely, professional designers attempt to create spatial orders when they design. We confront the issue of the designer's spatial orders versus those of the client.

chapters five and six: building with strategic vision

This brings us to a consideration of the design process through which designers, clients, and users forge a formal design. In dealing with spatial orders, deeply held values are at stake. Good designing must take place in a design process that sees these politicized interests and is inspired by a stragetic vision of the people and institution being designed for. In Chapter Five, we study these issues in three residential design case studies. In Chapter Six, we consider these issues in the design of three large institutions.

acknowledgments

THE patron of this book is Zick Rubin who requested and nurtured this manuscript through its four-year gestation, sensed the possibilities, and helped keep them alive.

I owe intellectual debts to the psychologists, sociologists, architects, planners, and design historians cited in the body of this book. In particular, Rudolf Arnheim incisively critiqued an early draft of this manuscript, which grounded and refreshed my thoughts. My friend and fellow architect, Murray Silverstein, read several early drafts, giving me the benefit of his encouraging and engaging intellectual companionship.

Over the past six years, numerous individuals have generously consented to interviews and allowed me into their spaces. I wish to thank them all, including Barbara Wright, the Boyles, Rusty Luethe, and Dr. Robert Edgar, as well as architects Don E. Olsen, Eugene Lew, Karl G. Smith, James Weber, William Turnbull, Aaron Green, and planner Mary Summers.

Jonathan Tsao, Floyd Tomkins, Marvin Buchanin, Martin Tornallyay, Venturi and Rauch, and others generously made photographs and illustrations available to me. At Prentice-Hall, Mike, Heath, Jeannette, Dawn, and Peter helped produce this book. I am responsible for the illustrations except where noted. My good friend Howard Menashe continued his role as critic-at-large. My sister, Linda Weingarten, gracefully translated Le Corbusier from French into English. And my wife Ruth often helped translate my text from typescript into English. This book is dedicated to her.

1

**romance with
space**

neutral versus acute space

Day to day, year after year, we carry on a romance with space. This romance leads us to seek our place and build on the face of the earth. We are in love with our spatial environments whether we are aware of it or not.

Our ordinary way of seeing space conceals this romance. Ordinarily, we consider our physical environments as neutral space. We think of space as a container for our activities, a supporting structure for lives proceeding independently of space. Architect Walter Gropius spoke about neutral space in these remarks on housing.

The problem of the minimum dwelling is that of establishing the elementary minimum of space, air, light and heat required by man in order that he be able to fully develop his life functions without experiencing restrictions due to his dwellings. . . .[1]

In neutral space, life and its physical environment are separated. In neutral space, we consider it best that the environment not impinge on life. We feel that environments have little to do with the real substance of our lives.

Despite neutral space, our space romance reveals itself periodically in acute, vivid, albeit brief interludes. Here our lives have a spatial feel. The boundaries between ourselves and our spatial contexts dissolve. Thus, a student wrote about his first solo flight at the controls of an airplane. For an instant, he experienced a union of himself and space.

I was impressed with the feeling of unlimited movement. The horizon seemed very distant, as did the ground below . . . I also experienced a sensation of infallibility— complete control without possible error in movement.[2]

Another young American was vividly immersed in space after a midnight escape across the Marmara Sea from a Turkish prison where he had been for five years. He was a free man on the beach to which he swam.

. . . I set off trotting toward the sun. The warm orange light gave me new strength. Ahead of me stretched the deserted

[1]Walter Gropius, *Scope of Total Architecture* (New York: Harper and Brothers, 1955), p. 113.

[2]Del Ray Maughan, Harvard College, 1970.

north coast of Asia Minor. This was the finest morning of my life.[3]

These acute space encounters have a framed quality to them. They have finite duration. We know while in them that we are not in ordinary, neutral space. In part, this framed quality stems from the vividness of acute space. We see spatial details clearly and freshly. Moreover, we see those details within the overall order of the moment, a moment in which issues of great importance to us are addressed.

Consider a romance that several of us had with the space of a small trailer-cabin in rural New Hampshire at sunset. The occasion was a wedding. Lisa and Steve, the bride and bridegroom, sat on the floor, their backs to the fireplace. The others, including Mike the host, Don the minister, and I, sat or stood around them. Everyone was sober—yet some of us entered acute space. Several weeks later, Lisa talked about her wedding. During the ceremony she had felt removed from normal reality. She felt no separation between what was happening to her and its spatial context. Her space included only herself and Steve. She felt herself and Steve encompassed in a special place just for themselves. When the ceremony ended, she experienced the framed quality of acute space. She experienced a return to the neutral space of Mike's cabin.

It felt like there was nobody else there, other than Steven and me. The minister was there, but he was different. He could have been a voice in the wall. I wasn't really relating to anyone as another person but Steve. (Q: Where did you feel you were? In open space?) Blankness, light blankness. I didn't see the room. I felt the room. I felt the smallness. It wasn't outside. It was sheltered, but it wasn't a big expanse. It was close. The wall was the edge. It was all that I could see. (Q: Why did you think Steve wanted to sit on the floor?) Evenness, like we could be right next to each other, like if we sat in two separate chairs, there would have been something between us. Also, like we were starting at the bottom. Of all the times I've kissed him, I think that that was a spiritual moment. I was really aware. (Q: Did your perception of the room change after you kissed?) Yea, I realized the room again. I realized that the wall was there, that the

[3]Billy Hayes with William Hoffer, *Midnight Express* (New York: Dutton, 1977), p. 253.

Franklin stove was starting. I looked at them. It became reality again. It was over then.

These acute immersions in space are a form of elementary spatial thinking. Items of importance to us are thought about concretely and spatially. The pilot saw broad, limitless expanses, the experience of unlimited freedom at his control. Lisa saw herself and Steve side by side starting out on ground level in a spatial place. Marriage for her was a beginning of two people together on the ground. Likewise, the groom saw himself in a universe that centered upon himself and that ordered his relationship to Lisa, to the rest of us in the room and to the rural woods he loved so much.

The wedding shined. It's hard to describe. I had a lot of energy. And I had my mind. Everything was clear. I could see everyone. Mike was taking pictures. Every once in a while a flash would come, wosh! And I knew where he was coming from. I thought of Lisa sitting next to me. I knew she was there. It was close. It was comfortable. I think my mind felt infinite and my body felt stronger. (Q: Did you think about the other parts of Mike's house?) Yea, because they were like the arms and the legs of the building. I could feel them. And you look around, the trees are outside and so I could feel the towers of the house. I don't know, it seemed like infinite, even with closed space, pretty infinite. I don't know, certain things like that make you touch your soul so your awareness opens.

Mike cared deeply for Steve and Lisa and enjoyed providing the space for their wedding. During the ceremony his acute space experience spoke to his basic detachment from the social conventions of marriage. Mike experienced the wedding through his camera's viewfinder. Taking pictures provided Mike with a way to involve himself at a distance from the ceremony itself.

The living room has a cave effect. I was getting outside the whole situation, you see. The light of the fireplace and the lanterns confined the wedding to the cave end. To take pictures was an "out-of-the-picture" type thing. You're out of it, and there it is, the whole thing in front of you!

Despite its brief duration, acute space has a profound impact on us. Acute space inspires us. It enters our experience and comments on something important and perhaps previously hidden. Afterward, it becomes a memory standing out in our recollections. Acute space focuses our attentions on important issues and moments. By vividly spatializing an important moment in our lives, acute space inspires us through time.

My recollections of the acute space of my own wedding have remained a vivid and rich memory of our marriage's basic roots and first hopes. As the two of us held hands barefoot and open to the ground at dawn, it seemed that we were suspended in time inside a magic circle. After the ceremony, we emerged from the glow of the circle in the darkness into daylight. What had felt like the magic circle was the outer edge of the circular putting green on which we were married at dawn. At Mike's cabin, I realized I had come to relive my own wedding. At first, I saw Steve and Lisa in the middle of the dark living room bathed in light from the candles and fireplace. But in the middle of the ceremony, I saw archetypal man and archetypal woman enshrined in colored light in dark space.

Warmth radiated out across the rug, disappearing into the dark surroundings where I was located and then out into the New Hampshire cold. As Steve and Lisa gave their vows and kissed, a fiery kind of light radiated from their bodies. Lisa was encircled in a light blue light, Steve in a light yellow light.

Despite these depictions, it is worth realizing that acute space is essentially invisible. It is experienced by its beholders. It cannot necessarily be seen by others looking at the same physical environment. Thus, Don—the minister—never entered acute space. He remained in neutral space. For Don the ceremony was a lovely event that never transcended its circumstances. Don remarked

We sat around for quite a while relaxed, having a conversation about a whole lot of things. And all of a sudden, Steve and Lisa sat right on the floor in front of me. They wanted it dark. I think that darkness always adds to the mood of the evening. But I needed that light by my chair so I could read the ceremony. It was physically very small. They were a foot or two away from me. They were right there, just because of the cramped construction of Mike's house.

the western denial   Our experience with acute space is rare. When it does occur, it is of limited duration. So we feel that the boundaries between ourselves and our physical environment do not dissolve every day. In fact, we may even deny that we can have any relationship with space apart from that which we have to neutral space.

Often we argue that it is only in exotic cultures that the me-versus-my-physical-environment boundary dissolves routinely. And we become fascinated by Black Elk, an Oglala Sioux medicine man, healing his people. For Black Elk, everyday life was a spatial drama.

You have noticed that everything an Indian does is in a circle, and that is because the Power of the World always works in circles . . . In the old days when we were a strong and happy people, all our power came to us from the sacred hoop of the nation, and so long as the hoop was unbroken, the people flourished . . . Birds make their nests in circles, for theirs is the same religion as ours. The sun comes forth and goes down again in a circle. The moon does the same, and both are round . . . Our teepees were round like the nests of birds, and these were always set in a circle, the nation's hoop, a nest of many nests, where the Great Spirit meant for us to hatch our children. But the [white man has] put us in these square boxes. Our power is gone and we are dying, for the power is not in us anymore.[4]

Architectural historian Vincent Scully studied the Pueblo Indians and wrote about a fundamental difference between Western and Pueblo architecture. Western culture descends from Greek culture, which in turn was based on a conception of human and nature separated yet balanced. But the Greeks acknowledged nature and we now ignore it. Scully observed that the American Indians are different. For them, there is no separation between life and its spatial context. Everything is alive and everything mirrors the world.

The American Indian world is a place where no conception whatever of any difference between men and nature can exist, since there is in fact no discrimination between nature

[4]John Neihardt, *Black Elk Speaks* (Lincoln, Neb.: University of Nebraska Press, 1961), pp. 198–200.

*and man as such, but only an ineradicable instinct that all
living things are one. And all are living . . .*[5]

Occasionally we learn about a "modern" people who dissolve the barriers between life and space on a daily basis. But we assure ourselves that these people are from unusual cultures far removed from our own. So, from a distance we may cherish stories of the Japanese tea ceremony.

In [*a tea house*] *garden the guests relax and free their
minds from the world's hubbub. After a short wait, the
guests move along the stepping-stones toward the tea hut
. . . The first guest enters alone and moves to the art alcove
where he inspects the scroll hung in honor of the occasion.
This scroll . . . helps establish the mood of the tea planned
by the host that day. Nearby is a single flower in a container.
These two objects are the only decorations in the room . . .
Like the garden around the hut, the tearoom reveals itself
only slowly. It is conducive to contemplation, and has already begun to do its work when the kettle begins to emit
the sound of boiling water . . . The host goes on making tea
for each guest in turn. His movement is clean and graceful,
with no interference between his thoughts and actions . . .
Nothing dramatic has happened . . . yet for a few minutes,
he has allowed his senses full reign, been part of an experience that unified sight, sound, smell, taste and touch.*[6]

This attitude, that we are fundamentally different from cultures in which space and life merge in the course of everyday life, has been given its definitive statement by Mircea Eliade. Western man and woman live by and large in neutral space, or what Eliade terms *profane space.* Here space is homogeneous. It is mapped and delineated. Yet all parts are considered qualitatively alike. For archaic man and woman, space is nonhomogeneous. Parts of it are qualitatively different from other parts. Some are sacred and of great significance to the religious person. Eliade called this *sacred space.* In sacred space, the world is alive and may invade and live through us. Hence, there are rites and prescriptions for how one builds and approaches sacred space. Eliade pointed out the alienation of modern man and woman from the experience of sacred space.

[5]Vincent Scully, *Pueblo: Mountain, Village, Dance* (New York: Viking Press, 1975), p. 9.

[6]Rand Castile, *The Way of Tea* (New York: Weatherhill, 1974), pp. 26–28.

Sacred and profane are two modes of being in the world, two existential situations assumed by man in the course of his history . . . The completely profane world, the wholly desacralized cosmos, is a recent discovery in the history of the human spirit . . . Desacralization pervades the entire experience of the nonreligious man of modern societies and, in consequence, he finds it increasingly difficult to re-discover the existential dimensions of religious man in the archaic societies.[7]

Despite these arguments and denials, the fact remains that even in our daily lives, we are not separated or detached from our spatial environments. Oblivious to them, we merge our everyday lives with space. Because we are looking at our own culture rather than at an interesting yet foreign culture, we cannot see how our understanding of everyday life is an understanding of everyday space. We cannot see that on a daily basis we spend a lot of time in chronic space.

chronic space   Chronic space is not an extraordinary space in the way that acute space is. Chronic space is the ordinary space of ordinary moments. One way to observe chronic space is to examine how we are annoyed or dissatisfied with aspects of our daily environment. Upon close examination, we find that correcting vaguely dissatisfying parts of everyday space seems to correct something in our lives. A student observed how he brought a sense of centeredness and calm into his life by the way in which he decorated his apartment.

In my bedroom study, I have emptied the center as much as possible. Beds and desks are no more than a foot off the floor. There is a heavy concentration of color on the walls and floor, all of which results in a remarkably peaceful environment.[8]

Another student wrote of a recurrent spatial wish. Every day while walking to classes, she kept daydreaming that her living quarters could somehow be located nearer the boys' quarters. She was dealing with her wishes and trepidations about coeducation through her daily spatial experience of walking to class.

[7]Mircea Eliade, *The Sacred and the Profane* (New York: Harcourt, Brace, Jovanovich, 1959), pp. 13–15.

[8]Richard Compton, Harvard College, 1970.

Over and over again, I was struck by the wish that the girls' library had never been built, so that the girls' college could simply move down to the boys' college. The idea was totally irrational though it recurred to me all the time.[9]

In both chronic and acute space, life issues are fused to space. The experience of space becomes an experience of the issues in one's life. Further, both chronic and acute space are essentially invisible to anyone other than the beholder; it was for that student alone to see the distance between the two colleges and thereby to experience the social separation that that implied for her. Yet there are distinctive differences between acute and chronic space. Unlike acute space, chronic space has an unframed quality. It recurs over and over. It does not have an explicit, finite duration. Chronic space does not seem especially vivid or dramatic to us. We slip back and forth between it and neutral space without being aware of any shift in the quality of our space experience. Chronic space feels normal. It takes careful reflection, observations, and outside help before we can see that chronic space is substantively different from neutral space.

Chronic space is manifest in ritual action as well as in spatial imagery. In ritual, our daily actions have consequences far beyond their direct impact. Ritual is not action repeated over and over in the course of life. Nor is any action ritual just because it is exotic or bizarre. What makes an action ritual is not the action itself but the context and consequences of it. In neutral space, action is instrumental and has explicit effects. But in chronic space, ritual has extended consequences. Ritual action manipulates chronic space and thereby manipulates life.

In the social science literature, ritual has been seen from several overlapping viewpoints. Anthropologist Mary Douglas considered ritual as a guide to perception.[10] Ritual focuses people's attention and controls their experience. Freud wrote that ritual was magic action.[11] Individuals develop rituals to ensure some kind of alteration of their lives.

[9]Debbie Hyde, Radcliffe College, 1970.

[10]Mary Douglas, *Purity and Danger* (Baltimore: Penguin Books, 1966), Chap. 4.

[11]Sigmund Freud, *A General Introduction to Psychoanalysis* (New York: Washington Square Press, 1960), Chap. 17.

Ritual is instrumental imagery. From our point of view, the imagery and ritual of chronic space are two sides of the same coin. Ritual is thought through action; imagery is action through thought. Both focus our attention onto life wedded to space. Both are instrumental attempts to guide our lives.

In chronic space, some rituals are simple. In neutral space, cleaning up one's house makes living in the house easier. Things can be found and stored quickly. But in chronic space, a cleaning ritual can renew one's life. Repositioning plants and furniture, dusting, making sure things are in the right order, and airing out the house reaffirms the order of life. One woman said

If I am depressed about whatever, one of the first things I'll do is clean up, make myself really feel good, namely make order with my life.

And another reported

Usually my husband and I will look at each other and feel really good and really enjoy waking up to a Saturday or Sunday morning with the place really clean. There is something sort of psychologically restful in having the place neat. Maybe it's like the autistic child who does not want things out of order.

Some rituals are more complex and coincide with more intricate, multirealm chronic spaces. Joseph paced back and forth from one realm of his apartment to another ostensibly to get food, watch television, or say hello to his wife in the course of an evening of heavy studying. His apartment consisted of two chronic space realms. His living-dining room and bedroom were a humane realm, a place of life with his wife and friends, a place full of the joy of his undergraduate years (Figure 1-1). His study at the opposite end of his apartment was a work realm tied to his strict career goals and rigid study schedules. He paced back and forth between his realms to assure himself of his commitment to both. Yet he wanted the separation between the realms to assure himself that neither would contaminate the other.

I guess I spend the majority of my waking hours in the study, but I take breaks fairly frequently, even though I shouldn't,

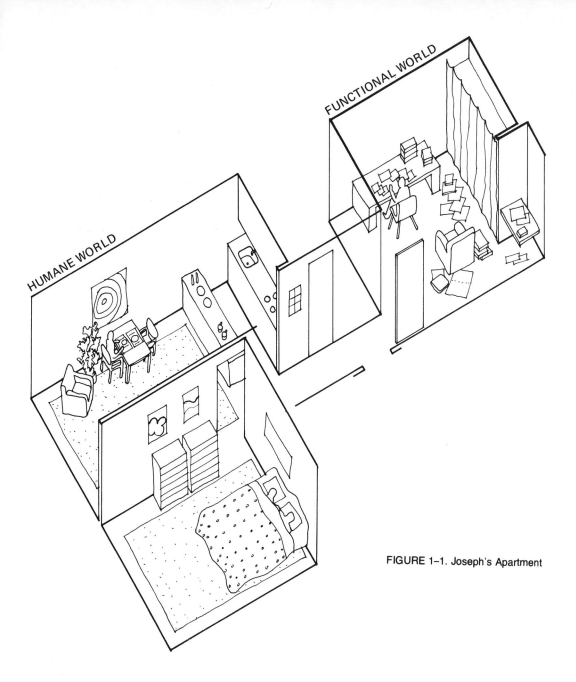

FIGURE 1–1. Joseph's Apartment

but I do. So I come in here, to the living room and bedroom. I open the study door, leave that world and come into this world. I'm a different personality in the study. (Q: Would you like this apartment if the bedroom were in back next to your study?) No, it would sort of combine my two worlds, which I personally wouldn't want to have happen.

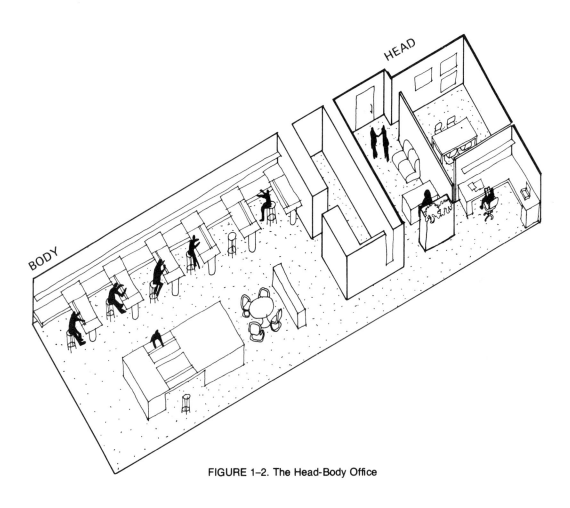

FIGURE 1–2. The Head-Body Office

In a similar vein, an architect built his office employing a spatial order creating "head" and "body" realms (Figure 1-2). The "head" contained a small foyer with secretary, a conference room, and the architect's private office. The rest of the staff occupied a large room of the "body"— connected by a narrow "neck" to the "head." This architect prided himself on a practice in which intellectual strategy and insight directed the labor of his staff. He would often come speeding into the "body," giving the staff lightning directives, creating work for the staff. The secretary and some of the staff felt cut off from each other. They suggested more connection and more openings between the realms. But the architect insisted that the two areas had to be separate.

We have been introduced to acute and chronic space with their similar yet complementary qualities. Acute space is vivid, standing out from the rest of our experience. Yet acute space is short-lived and relatively rare. It has largely inspirational power. We return to our memories of acute space to ponder the questions posed for us there. These memories guide, remind, and reassure us of things that seem important. On the other hand, chronic space is recurrent. We can spend considerable time in it over the course of a week. Chronic space feels ordinary and mundane, yet it has immense impact on our lives. It pervades daily life, directing how we tidy up, how we decide to move about, and how we spend money on our environments.

Acute and chronic space are manifestations of human intelligence. They provide us with ways of identifying, reflecting on, and acting on important issues in life. In this way, acute and chronic space form a basis for thinking about the course of life spatially. In our lifelong romance with space, we immerse ourselves in our environments and in the process learn to build a world for our lives.

the intelligence of space

2

spatial orders

We have discussed the acute and chronic experiences in which the content of our lives is folded into space. This space experience is the basis by which we evolve visions of how our physical environments must be built. Now we must investigate the processes that shape our experiences of acute and chronic space. Later we will discuss how we take such experiences and develop them further into spatial visions—or "spatial orders"—governing how we select and build physical environments.

learning and thinking with space

We are trained to see space in subtle ways. Consider neutral space, the space-as-container, space-as-separate-from-life experience already discussed. Psychologists have studied how we are trained by our everyday activities to see neutral space.

In the 1920s, psychologist Grace de Laguna argued that what we see is shaped by how we are rewarded in seeing.[1] In her analysis, an infant learns to discriminate the orchestration of open and closed doors, hallway paths, and cupboard locations as they relate to a reward—cookies in a jar, for instance. These are "secondary objects" that the child learns in the process of obtaining rewarding "primary objects." The learning of secondary objects constitutes learning neutral space.

De Laguna's work suggested that people living in fundamentally different environments learn to see space differently. Segall, Campbell, and Herskovits argued just this point in their study of cross-cultural differences in space perception.[2] They predicted that people who grew up in environments with flat, planar buildings at right angles to each other—what the authors called a "carpentered world"—are susceptible to different visual-spatial illusions than people who grow up in noncarpentered environments. The carpentered world teaches its occupants that horizontals receding to a vanishing point are indications of great distance (Figure 2-1a). In the carpentered world, the reced-

[1]Grade de Laguna, *Speech: Its Function and Development* (Bloomington, Ind.: Indiana University Press, 1963), Chap. IX. Also, B. F. Skinner, *About Behaviorism* (New York: Knopf, 1974), Chap. 5.

[2]M. H. Segall, D. T. Campbell, and M. J. Herskovits, *Cultural Influences on Visual Perception* (Indianapolis: Bobbs-Merrill, 1966), and "Cultural Differences in the Perception of Geometric Illusions," *Science* 139 (1963), 169–177.

ing horizontals of Figure 2-1b indicate an object at close range. The spatial environment of noncarpentered worlds, for instance, a circular mud hut village, would not train its occupants to make these discriminations. The authors presented the two-dimensional Müller-Lyre illusion to a wide sampling of subjects. They asked the subjects which horizontal line (in Figure 2-2a or in Figure 2-2b) was longer. Carpentered world subjects consistently stated that the line in Figure 2-2a was longer, even when it was equal or slightly less long than the line in Figure 2-2b. These subjects read the horizontal of Figure 2-2a as longer because it looked to be at a greater distance from the subject, and hence to be of greater apparent length. Noncarpentered world subjects were not susceptible to this illusion. They were not influenced by the learned depth inference of receding horizontals.

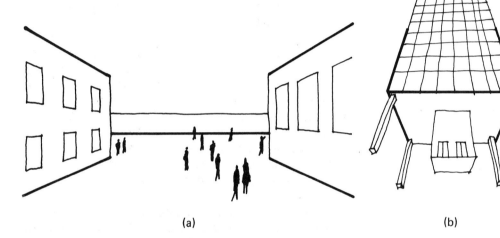

(a)   (b)

FIGURE 2–1 (*above*). (a) "Carpentered World—Angular Lines Receding to a Large Distant Horizontal, (b) "Carpentered World"—Angular Lines Approaching a Close-up Horizontal of Relatively Small Length

FIGURE 2–2 (*below*). The Müller-Lyre Illusion—In Which One Is the Horizontal Line Longer?

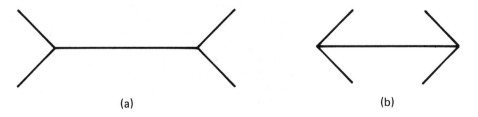

(a)   (b)

In Western cultures, studies have suggested that people differ among themselves in the way that they see their cities.[3] If daily activities require people to coordinate their impressions of a city, they learn an overall, coherent image of it. If their activities make no such demands, they have a more fragmentary, uncoordinated image of their city.

Just as we are trained to see neutral space, we are also trained to see space that is folded into our lives. Moment to moment, we engage in social situations shaped by subliminal rules.[4] In learning these rules, we learn to experience space socially. We are trained to associate particular social nuances with particular impressions of space. In childhood, our homes and schools subtly train us to distinguish places in which our activities are well structured versus improvisational. Familiar and more structured social situations are likely to occur around a dining table or up front in a classroom. Less structured and more improvisational situations are likely in the home entry or in the school stairways. Bruno Bettelheim sought to include a balance of structured and improvisational spaces in his school for emotionally disturbed children.[5] He had found that some children remain in structured, well-mastered situations out of a fear of changing situations. These children need experience in less definite, in-between spaces. They need experience with situational transition. Yet he had also found that too much time in in-between spaces results in a child's withdrawal from participation in the structured classroom.

An analysis of acute space experience can reveal the variety of training that helped shape it. Consider the acute space that I experienced when my friend Eric and I hiked out of a valley on a hot Fourth of July. Eric had been a Zen student, and this was my first opportunity to talk at length

[3]George Rand, "Pre-Copernican Views of the City," *Architectural Forum* (September 1969), pp. 76–81, and Donald Appleyard, "Styles and Methods of Structuring a City," *Environment and Behaviour,* 2 (1970), 100–117.

[4]The term *social situation* is used in the sense meant by W. I. Thomas in "The Four Wishes and the Definition of the Situation," in *Theories of Society,* eds. Talcott Parsons, and others (New York: Free Press, 1961), or in the sense of "interaction" or "encounters" used by Erving Goffman in *The Presentation of Self in Everyday Life* (Garden City, N.Y.: Doubleday Anchor, 1959), or in the sense of "gathering" used by Goffman in *Behavior in Public Places* (New York: Free Press, 1963).

[5]Bruno Bettelheim, *Love is Not Enough* (New York: Collier Books, 1965), Chap. 5.

with him about his practice. I had looked forward to our encounter.

Going up the steep slopes, our conversation became entangled. Eric made a few comments that quieted the entanglement. As we neared the ridge, walking became easier and conversation flowed more freely. There was a moment of powerful insight just as we reached the top of the ridge. Suddenly I could see down into the valley we had just climbed out of. I could see miles ahead over neighboring mountains out to San Francisco and the Pacific Ocean.

This was a memorable experience for me, this sudden, vast spatial and intellectual panorama following the darkness and obscurity of the valley below.

Eric and I were in a two-person social situation. Our movements were controlled by subcultural rules of social situations. As in all social situations, ours had an inclusion concern, namely, how to establish appropriate communication channels between us. Inclusion concerns require a spatial solution. To stand two feet apart, we could have seen each other's minute facial expressions and embraced. At fifteen

FIGURE 2–3. Briones Park, California

Photo: Glenn Lym

feet, such detailed body communications would be impossible. Only the broadest body gestures and loud, simple phrases could be picked up.[6] Both of these distances were inappropriate to our situation. So we began our conversation walking side by side, turning to face each other at three feet apart, the social-acquaintance distance for conversation. But as we climbed up the mountain, the path became steep and narrow. We had to walk single file and could no longer maintain our three-foot distance. To compensate for this disturbance to our communication, we raised our voices and walked slowly enough to hear each other. Near the summit, we could resume our side by side, three-foot distance. And at the top, we stood farther apart, reflecting on what had been said, not needing to talk further. Social situations are also goverened by exclusion concerns. Eric and I were accompanied on our walk by other friends. Our conversation was intimate and could not handle the intrusion of other conversations. So we placed distance between ourselves and the others and walked so that the others were either ahead of us or behind us.

By controlling spatial movement, the rules of social situations controlled how we saw space. As Eric and I approached the hill, we talked comfortably side by side. And in between our talk, we could glance about at the land and dry grasses. But as the hill got steeper when our conversation got entangled, we had to walk single file up a steep hill and adjust our voices loud enough to hear each other, yet not so loud as to communicate to our friends in front and in back of us. So going up the hill became tedious, and there was little time to survey the land. I felt cramped socially and spatially. As we reached the ridgetop, we could fall back to our side by side positions. The space of our conversation loosened up. And when we reached the top, our conversation was over and we were free fully to observe the views and space around us.

In a similar manner, the rules of social situations also shape our experiences of chronic space. Consider Joan's apartment (Figure 2-4). She felt that her apartment was segregated into two realms, her husband's study and the rest of the apartment where she spent her time. She felt that her husband's closed study door helped create this fragmenta-

---

[6]These are part of the analysis of proxemics in Edward T. Hall, *The Hidden Dimension* (Garden City, N.Y.: Doubleday, 1966).

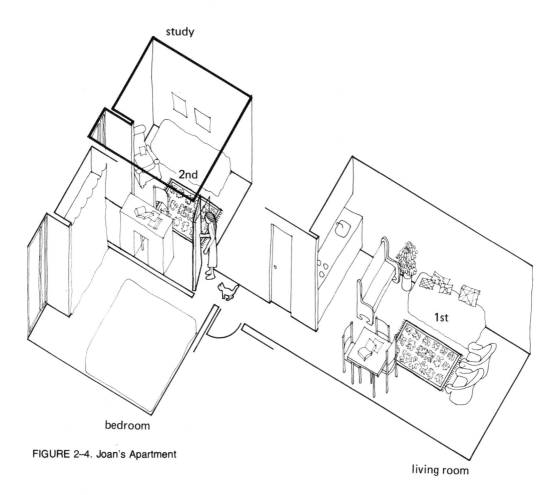

study

2nd

bedroom

FIGURE 2–4. Joan's Apartment

1st

living room

tion of her apartment. She wanted her apartment to feel whole; she wanted to feel her husband's realm included in her apartment space. Her husband's study had been open to the rest of the apartment until Joan and her husband had purchased a fine Oriental rug. They had first placed it in their living room in a communal area adjacent to her own study area at the dining table. But their cat started pulling on the rug. The husband got upset, picked up the rug, placed it in his study, and closed the study door, saying he was keeping the cat away from the rug (Figure 2-4). In time, Joan formulated a door opening ritual.[7] She felt that it was unfair to deny herself and the cat access to the whole apartment. So she opened the study door to make herself feel whole again.

[7]For a discussion of ritual, see Chapter 1.

45466

When my husband is not home, I open the study door, even though I know the cat will go in and pull up on the rug. I just leave it open and that way the study becomes a part of the apartment.

Joan's husband considered rug appreciation to be a one-person situation. He had always envisioned a study for himself complete with Oriental rug. But to do so, he had to exclude the cat who would destroy the rug. He used a physical exclusion prop—his closed study door.[8] Joan wanted rug appreciation to be a two-person situation or her own one-person situation. Either way, her situation required the use of the door for inclusion through her open door ritual. Competing definitions of rug appreciation led the husband to close his door. This cut Joan off from his study and the rug. This in turn led her to focus on the door as a means for rug inclusion. These inclusion and exclusion concerns shaped Joan's experience of her apartment space.

In acute and chronic space experiences, our rules of social situations operate upon events of importance to us in a manner that lets us see what is happening in a special way—in a spatial way. In acute and chronic space experience, social situationally-shaped impressions of space enable us to feel out, react to, and record critical portions of our lives, as was the case in my valley walk, Joan's door closing ritual, and the experiences of the pilot and wedding participants discussed in Chapter One.

We should not take this situationally guided seeing too lightly. The seeing that takes place in acute and chronic space experience is not simply a passive absorption of disconnected facts out of our lives. This situational seeing is itself a creative act. At first this might seem odd to you. Psychologists have long considered that the seeing that takes place in the presence of the thing seen is a passive perception of an external world. This seeing has been considered an inferior form of thought-inhibiting abstraction. Goldstein and Scheerer wrote that thinking through images

---

[8]For this distinction between prop versus body resolutions of situational demands, see Irwin Altman and E. E. Lett, "The Ecology of Interpersonal Relationship: a Classification System and Conceptual Model," in *Social and Psychological Factors in Stress*, ed. J. E. McGrath (New York: Holt, Rinehart and Winston, 1970).

of the world limits intelligence.[9] Jerome Bruner argued that children who think by using images are locked into a superficial understanding of their world.[10] He concluded that thinking by imagery binds thought to the observable rather than to the essential character of events.

Napoleon is reported to have said that men who think in images are not fit to command . . . It is only when [the child] can go beyond this [imagery]. . . . that he comes to deal with such nonsensory ideas as the relations between quantities . . .[11]

In contrast, psychologists have considered that pure imagination or thinking in the absence of the thing seen is a powerful form of thought. Bruner wrote that the visual imagination of the artist has the power of efficient connection. Seemingly disparate items can be visually connected, resulting in new and poignant experience.

To combine man with horse in the image of the centaur is to connect the image of man's rational gift with a renewed image of virility . . . An image is created connecting things that were previously separate in experience . . . It is precisely in its economy that art shares a fundamental principle with other forms of knowing . . . The principle of economy in art produces the compact image or symbol that, by its genius, travels great distances to connect ostensible disparities.[12]

As Freud discovered, we all create powerful images in our sleep. Our more elaborate dreams display the skill and economy of means attributed to Bruner's artist. In dreams, multiple meanings are condensed into efficient, connected images. Some years back, I had a dream in a period of my life when I was in transition from my social science studies back into design. At the time, of course, I was unaware of this transition. In the dream

[9]Kurt Goldstein and Martin Scheerer, "Abstract and Concrete Behavior," *Psychological Monographs,* 53: 239.

[10]Jerome S. Bruner, and others, *Studies in Cognitive Growth* (New York: John Wiley, 1966).

[11]Bruner, *Studies in Cognitive Growth,* pp. 28–29.

[12]Jerome S. Bruner, *On Knowing: Essays for the Left Hand* (New York: Atheneum, 1962), pp. 62–65.

I was in a large cubic-shaped building. It was on fire. Its interior ramps and bridges were burning. I fled the building and embarked on a journey that took me to a city's downtown, then off into a wonderful park with a music shed where I stayed. But I moved on only to find myself standing in front of that large building again. It was still on fire, but now the fire was a dancing yet vital fire. I entered the building.

This dream had at least three levels of meaning. First, it dealt with my feelings that architecture produced lifeless buildings. Later, I came to see architecture as something alive with a burning spirit. Second, the dream referred to my need to get away from design in order to see it from its context—to get away from the building and find it anew. Third, the dream made reference to my having left design in order to preserve myself. For my own safety, I left the burning building. Later, I would return, several years after this dream, now drawn in by the life energy of design itself. In my dream as in other dreams, spatial and visual devices state multiple meanings powerfully and succinctly. A fire can be both destructive and life embodying, or a building can be fled from and then anxiously returned to.

To come back to our argument, the seeing in acute and chronic space—the seeing in the presence of the thing seen—is not a passive or an inferior form of intelligence with respect to pure imagination. Rudolf Arnheim has pointed out that thinking divested of sensory contact is itself limited. He argued that intelligence connected to immediate circumstances is a necessary condition for thinking. Seeing tied to the observable does not confine thought but grounds it in reality and grounds reality in a critical perspective.

Traditionally, abstraction is a withdrawal from direct experience. This view assumes a dichotomy between perceiving and thinking . . . [But] perception and thinking cannot get along without each other . . . To rephrase Kant's pronouncement: vision without abstraction is blind; abstraction without vision is empty . . . If one asserts that abstraction requires withdrawal, one risks subjecting the mind to conditions under which thinking cannot function; one will also fail to acknowledge genuine thinking when it is concerned with problems posed by direct experience.[13]

[13]Rudolf Arnheim, *Visual Thinking* (Berkeley: University of California Press, 1969), pp. 188–189.

The seeing of acute and chronic space experience has precisely these attributes of abstraction amid immediate circumstances discussed by Arnheim. Yet, this seeing also has the characteristic of condensed, multiple levels of meaning found in pure imagination. In going up the hill with Eric, my situationally shaped impressions of space formed a whole image. Going up the hill became a journey from tedious effort to clarity at the top—a journey from confusion in the valley to insight and overview at the top. Joan's situational impressions of her apartment focused on the rug, the study door, and her confinement to a portion of her apartment. Her chronic space seeing incorporated these impressions into an image of her apartment divided into two separate realms seeking to be whole again.

Up to now we know that acute and chronic space experiences are derived from important social situations. We know that the dynamics of those situations shape our attention to space. Social inclusion and exclusion require spatial solutions solved by body movement and physical props. This in turn controls our spatial movements, thereby shaping our experience of space and giving situational meaning to space. The seeing formed from these situational constraints is concise and often multilayered in meaning. Far from being a passive reporting of mere events in our lives, acute and chronic space seeing root our thinking about our lives into our worldly circumstances.

Acute and chronic space experiences are gems of insight. We do not let them pass along the wayside. We use them as the elements from which we develop our visions for how our spaces and thus our lives can be built.

symbol formation and spatial orders

Acute space experiences may be developed into what psychologist Carl Jung termed a *symbol*. To Jung, a symbol captures more than its obvious meaning. A symbol captures material in the unconscious.[14] A symbol has charisma, preoccupying people over an extended period of time. It becomes a guide by which people rethink their lives. The symbol presents important unconscious material seeking expression in and integration with our conscious-

[14]Carl Jung, *Man and His Symbols* (Garden City, N.Y.: Doubleday, 1964), and Jung, "On Psychic Energy: Symbol Formation," in *The Collected Works of C. J. Jung,* vol. 8 (Princeton, N.J.: Princeton University Press, 1969).

FIGURE 2–5. Jung's Stone at Bollingen

Photo: Aniela Jaffe, Zurich, from *Memories, Dreams, Reflections* by C. J. Jung, Random House, 1961

ness. Jung told of his own experience with symbol formation in his account of carving a four-square, cubic stone at his vacation home in Bollingen (Figure 2-5).

I began to see on the front face . . . a sort of eye, which looked at me. I chiseled it into the stone . . . a tiny homunculus . . . yourself—which you see in the pupil of another's eye . . . The stone stands outside my house at Bollingen and is like an explanation of it . . . The stone reminded me of Merlin's life in the forest . . . Men still hear his cries . . . but they cannot understand nor interpret them. . . .[15]

Acute space experiences become symbols for their beholders. These experiences stake out time, places, and immediate events, signaling to the beholders that something special has happened. Later, the beholders can return to their memory of a vivid, acute space and come to know its full message. My hike with Eric was a continual source of insight into my expectations and misunderstandings about Zen practice. Returning to its imagery, I realized that the space of that hike was an understanding of a path from confusion to panoramic simplicity. Another acute

[15]Carl Jung, *Memories, Dreams, Reflections* (New York: Pantheon, 1961), pp. 226–228.

space experience became a symbol of my sense of occupation and home. One spring in New Hampshire, I was out for a drive, when my van became stuck in the deep mud created by the melting snows.

I got out and walked through the mud down the road, as if in a dream. I waded across a stream and onto a paved cross-road. There, across the road was a small, modern ranch-style house set among trimmed lawns, quite a sight in the country wilds. A young couple occupied this house. They hustled a special line of soap and home products, decorating their walls and refrigerator door with pictures of luxurious objects that they were intent on purchasing. No one was home. Further up the road I came across a plywood imitation of an old New England house. A retired Boston couple of some pretentions lived here. Their telephone was placed amid old photographs of the wife's show business career. Yet this elderly couple did not want me to wait for the tow truck at their house. I retraced my steps, passing the soap hustlers' home again and, a mile later, came upon an old white house built in the 1880s beside a bubbling stream. An old lady lived here, invited me in, and served me coffee, while she baked in her wood-burning stove. I was comfortable and waited for the tow truck. The young couple could not help me. The pretentious older couple gave help begrudgingly. But the old woman gave help, shelter, and warmth. I was aware of the architecture of these three groups. The young couple had a house that gestured toward suburban comfort, but was artificial in its rural context. The retired couple had a fake New England colonial house turned backward on its site. It was comfortable but exclusive. The old woman had a genuine New England house and offered true hospitality. Days later, as I thought more about this experience, I realized that it was a parable for my life at the time. I was stuck at a crossroads. There were several choices I had in establishing a home and occupation. There was the young, economically exploitive couple straight ahead, the elderly, artificial urban transplants, or the old New Hampshire lady. I had found my choice, a house built in relationship to its land offering genuine hospitality.

Symbol formation in chronic space takes a different form than symbol formation in acute space. Chronic space has none of the framed qualities of acute space. If we were aware of our own chronic space experiences, we could dwell on them and pick them over for insight into our lives, as we do with acute space experiences. But we do not do this. Instead, we slowly create spatial visions out of our most important chronic space experiences, visions of how our world should be built. These visions, or spatial orders, are the symbols of chronic space.

Chronic space experience needs spatial orders to survive. Spatial orders specify the optimal settings for continuing our chronic space experience. This is especially important as we often make chronic space out of a changing variety of homes, work places, and cities. Spatial orders help us determine what to rent or buy or visit in a way such that our spaces remain infused with our lives.

Joan, with her chronic open door ritual, had had this ritual in a previous apartment as well. There her husband had kept a valued air-conditioner rather than an Oriental rug in his study. And there, too, she wanted her husband's study to become part of her own space and would open the door to it on hot days when he was not home. In both apartments she had a special area adjacent to a communal space for her own studying, yet invariably she would move her work to the dining table and commence open study door rituals to include her husband's study into her own world. She had distilled the essence of her chronic space of home into a spatial order. When asked about what she wanted in an ideal house, Joan stated her vision. She wanted a house with many levels inside that were not all walled off. Her spatial order of a home totally accessible to her guided how she set up her apartments and what she expected in her future housing. Her spatial order captured her desire for personal wholeness through her occupancy of everything that she thought was hers within her apartment.

In Chapter One, we saw how Joseph maintained contact between home chronic realms by ritually pacing back and forth between his functional study world and his humane living room-bedroom world. From his experience of the chronic space of his apartment, Joseph had evolved a spatial order to guide his future geographic movements and the construction of his dream house. His spatial order preserved his distinction between his functional and humane worlds, yet set up a path to lead him from a functional world back, in the end, to his humane world. Joseph wanted a path from a functional, work-oriented life in New York City back to an elegant, humane world somewhat like his undergraduate days in Cambridge, Massachusetts.

I will move to New York for a few years, sort of making my fortune in New York and then come back up here, forget all about business and law, and go back to school. Possibly I'll become a teacher in something or other, in a more humane subject. I'd love to study music and art. In ten years, I would like to be living in Cambridge again. I would like to have made my fortune in the world and come back.

This conception of a humane world derived from the chronic space of his wood-paneled undergraduate college days. His future retirement home would be an elaboration of his humane world devoid of a functional realm.

I'd like to have a very old house. I conceive of a big library just filled with all sorts of books, heavy oak and heavy paneling, having a roaring fire and high ceilings.

The spatial orders or symbols that we form from our chronic space experience reach across time and distance. In our spatial orders, we evaluate and try out the implications of chronic space experiences. Spatial orders enable us to preserve and improve the quality and content of our chronic experiences.

3

**the spatial
order of the
home**

Our homes are a unique class of environments that are heavily saturated in chronic space experience. From our day-to-day experience with home space, we evolve spatial orders for home. These orders distill our sense of who we are, what we are made of, and how we relate to others around us. It is these spatial orders that form the basis by which we select and build new living spaces for ourselves. And in establishing homes throughout our lives, we enter into a dialogue with space. We come to shape ourselves as we shape our homes. Through our spatial orders of home, we engage ourselves in a lifelong process of self-discovery.

Our spatial orders of home have two aspects—an internal order and an external order. The internal order contends with the multitude of "faces" that a person wears. The internal order takes the collection of activities, objects, and places that comprise who we are and gives that collection an order. In this way, the internal order of the home is an ordering of our sense of self. The external order of home also deals with how we see ourselves, but with respect to the larger, less intimate, outside world. The external order defines us by locating our home with respect to important categories of people and places. The external order is an ordering of ourselves in terms of the public and the landscape.

In this chapter, we will first consider the internal order of home, then the external order. And then we will look at the succession of homes that architect Frank Lloyd Wright built for himself.

the internal order of the home

The internal order of the home establishes priorities and organizes our spatial experience of our home. Like all spatial orders, the home spatial order identifies space experience that is crucial to our experience of ourselves.

Sometimes we formulate a home spatial order that defines us in a way that we want to hold on to. Freud once discussed a young girl with just such a neurotic, mini home spatial order.[1] This girl did not want her parents to conceive a second child that would rival her. She wanted to prevent that birth. So she developed a spatial order in which she

[1]Sigmund Freud, *A General Introduction to Psychoanalysis* (New York: Washington Square Press, 1960), Chap. 17.

insisted on having her bedroom door open, enabling her to monitor her parents (Figure 3-1). Her room had to be arranged in a painstaking manner.

Her bolster could not touch the wooden bedstead at the head of the bed. Her pillow had to fit as a diamond across the bolster. Her head had to be placed exactly in the center of this pillow. And the eiderdown had to be shaken down so that its stuffing sank to the bottom. She shook the eiderdown several times before she was satisfied. All this took her two hours to perform.

FIGURE 3–1. The Bedtime Ritual of Freud's Patient

Through therapy, Freud helped the girl understand the meaning of her spatial order. In wanting to preserve her exclusive relationship to her parents, she thought of the bed bolster as a woman and the upright bedback as a man. By keeping them separate, she ritually kept her parents apart. Shaking the eiderdown so that a bump was made at its bottom meant to her impregnating a woman. So she would reshake the eiderdown again and again, obliterating the pregnancy only to reimpregnate the woman-eiderdown. The little pillow was herself resting on her mother, the bed bolster. The pillow was placed diamond-shaped on the bolster signifying female genitals. And the placement of her body and head onto that diamond signified the male genitals. In her spatial order, she imposed herself between her mother and her father. Freud's patient used her home spatial order to solidify and preserve a desperate and essentially untenable conception of herself.

More often than not, we formulate home spatial orders that explore and expand our sense of ourselves. Sometimes we do this by ingesting the world into our homes and thereby formulating new aspects of ourselves. This was the case with Clarence Schmidt, who found himself stuck in New York City life. One day he decided to leave and move to rural Woodstock, New York. His house building was guided by spatial orders that absorbed events happening in the world around him and thereby defined himself and his home in terms of those events. He scavenged Woodstock garbage cans for parts for his house. Visitors often brought him presents of old dishes, broken mirrors, or old car parts. Schmidt never turned down these gifts. He always created a place for them. Inside his house, there were rooms lined with bits of old mirrors and tables of wood covered with silver foil. There were used silver and white Christmas trees and silvered pots containing fake purple flowers next to painted baby dolls, all tied together by links of old Christmas tree lights. These were rooms that one visitor described as "musty, silent, grotto-like, some filled with brilliant colored lights." Outside, Schmidt created gardens. There were evergreen trees whose lower branches were covered with silver foil. Some trees were stuffed with the arms and legs of baby dolls. Sunlight and moonlight seemed to emanate from the trees. A wooden shed was ornamented with automobile steering wheels and grills as well as mirrors and painted pieces of old fence lumber. It, too, shone with beams of light (Figure 3-2).

Schmidt's house eventually rose up the mountain for seven floors and contained thirty-six rooms and many passages. People who have talked with Schmidt recall his long explanations of how he captured events and forces around him by creating obscure geometries of rocks, pots, and pictures. When John Kennedy died, Schmidt built a memorial to the Kennedy family. Faces and hands were arranged in a crucifix. When his house reached its full height and joined with the mountain top, he made a roof garden—the Garden of Eden in its last moments of pleasure before the fall.

Deep within the home, adjacent to a totally dark room, was the "inner sanctum" where Schmidt ate, watched television, and slept. Next to the house, he built a bridge. He stayed in the treehouse when the climate was severely cold or perhaps when he wanted to be removed from the forces of his home. When Schmidt was at home, he was in chronic space. His home ingested the forces that he saw in the world. He gave those forces an order and, in the process, brought himself in line with their power.

FIGURE 3–2. Schmidt House, Woodstock, New York

Photo: Beryl Sokoloff

The home spatial order can explore and define ourselves in a less worldly and more introspective manner. In the case of Jung's countryside home, we find such a spatial order that slowly evolved as he evolved. Jung started to build in 1923. He bought land by the side of a lake at Bollingen, Switzerland, and, like Schmidt, took four decades to complete his house. Jung found that building the house was a voyage in self-discovery.

FIGURE 3–3 (a to e). The Evolution of Jung's House at Bollingen

FIGURE 3–3a. 1923, A Maternal Realm

It gave me a feeling as if I were being reborn in stone . . . During the building work, of course, I never considered these matters . . . Only afterward did I see how all the parts fitted together and that a meaningful form had resulted; a symbol of psychic wholeness.[2]

Jung was continually unaware of his home spatial order. As he said, he would build and only later discover what he had built. The first phase of his house was a two-story tower (Figure 3-3a). His mother had just died. He found that the tower was a retreat and a place of rejuvenation beside a fireplace. Later, Jung realized that he had created a maternal realm.

[2]Carl Jung, *Memories, Dreams, Reflections* (New York: Pantheon, 1961), p. 225.

I . . . had in mind an African hut where the fire . . . burns in the middle and the whole life of the family revolves around this center . . . The feeling of repose and renewal . . . was intense from the start. It represented for me the maternal hearth. But I became increasingly aware that . . . something was still lacking . . . so, four years later, in 1927, the central structure was added (Figure 3-3b).[3]

FIGURE 3–3b. 1927, Central Structure

Jung was troubled with this central structure. Although he would eventually refocus his attentions on it, he felt that his home was incomplete. So four years later, he added a third construction, a tower annex, which contained a room where he could be by himself, away from family and friends (Figure 3-3c). This tower captured his spiritual aspects.

I wanted a room in this tower where I could exist for myself alone . . . carried out of time into seclusion, out of the present into timelessness . . . [This] tower became for me a place of spiritual concentration.[4]

[3]Ibid., pp. 223–224.
[4]Ibid., p. 224.

FIGURE 3–3c. 1931, Spiritual Tower

In 1935, again four years after his last addition to Bollingen, Jung felt the need to build once more. He sensed his house as a composition of three parts, the maternal tower, the central structure, and the spiritual tower. He felt the need to create a fourth part of the house that would be open to nature, yet fenced in. He built a courtyard and loggia by the lake (Figure 3-3d), and then stopped building.

Jung's wife died twenty years later, in 1955. Once again, he felt a need to find his central, true self. In the midst of his maternal and spiritual towers, he rediscovered his home's central tower. He found a new reordering of the places that were his home and built one more time (Figure 3-3e).

I felt an inner obligation to become what I myself am . . . I suddenly realized that the small central section which crouched so low, so hidden, was myself! I could no longer hide myself behind the "maternal" and the "spiritual" towers . . . I added an upper story to this section, which represents myself, or my ego-personality. [5]

[5]Ibid., p. 225.

FIGURE 3–3d. 1935, The Fourth Addition

FIGURE 3–3e. 1955, Discovered Central Self

Jung anticipated knowing himself through his home. He depended on uncovering his evolving spatial order of home and thereby becoming conscious of his evolving self.

The Schmidt and Jung homes are fantastic houses, quite unlike those in which most of us live. But the glamor or size of these homes should not mislead us into thinking that our own homes are any different. In point of fact, the same processes that shaped the Schmidt and Jung homes shape the homes of those who neither design nor build their housing. Spatial orders can just as easily create home out of and define us in a rented apartment as out of new construction.

Barbara lived for several years in the rented apartment in Cambridge, Massachusetts, pictured in Figure 3-4. She had divorced her husband and was a working woman, preferring to live alone with her children, except for the occasional visits of boyfriends. In her small and messy apartment, she evolved a unique home. In what normally would have been a living room, Barbara developed a children's bedroom and a large play area complete with wooden jungle gym. The middle room at first remained unused. It was furnished by the landlord with some chairs and a sofa with a broken spring (this state of the middle room is not pictured in Figure 3-4). Barbara made the little room off the middle room her own room. She felt that the bedroom and the kitchen were the core of her home. In the kitchen, she distinguished two distinct places. One was around her dining table, where she held forth with friends and neighbors who dropped by for coffee, food, good long chats, arguments, and fun. The other place was the open floor area in the kitchen that would fill with children at play while the grownups talked around the table. Barbara's front door was rarely used. Most people entered by the rear door, directly into the kitchen.

In time, Barbara noticed a change in her life. She had found neighbors among whom she felt comfortable. She was happy as a mother, yet wanted another daughter. So she began adoption proceedings. Barbara was also troubled about political commitments, her commitment to her boyfriends and her commitment to her career. To help her chances for adoption, she decided to make a presentable living room out of her middle room to impress the adoption case workers. She bought a good, used sofa, a new chair,

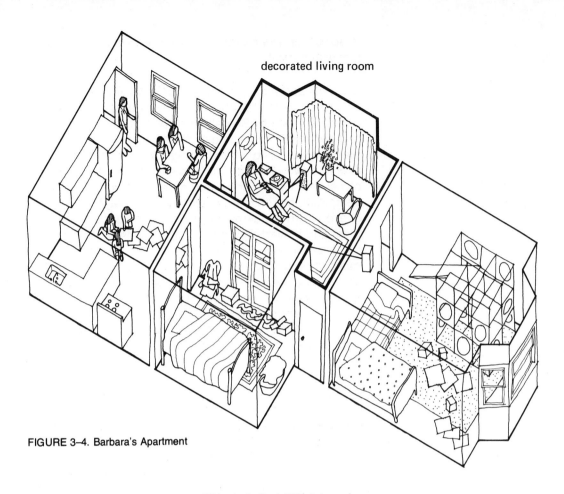

decorated living room

FIGURE 3–4. Barbara's Apartment

and new curtains for the room (Figure 3-4). A little later, she bought a stereo. She required toys to be picked up in this room, so that it was tidy and felt clean at special times. She discovered that she liked to sit in the new chair. Now, when her home was quiet, she would suggest moving from the kitchen to the new middle room to have a cup of tea. She would sit in her chair and relish its atmosphere. Barbara felt that her kitchen table was a place of "active public life." She thought of her new middle room during tea as a place of "passive public life," the only such place in her home.

Barbara's tea drinking was a chronic space ritual that went back to her high school years when she used to stay up late and study. Her mother would come home very late from work and prepare tea for the two of them. It was a time for mother and daughter to be alone and to talk. In her apartment, Barbara now drank tea in her new room as she waited to adopt her new daughter, making a quiet and fuller contact with herself.

In a year and a half, Barbara received her new child, quit her old job to spend time with her two daughters, and then began a new job. She altered her political commitments and decided to buy a house down the street. Although the plaster was falling off its ceilings, she liked it and knew exactly how to set it up. The house enabled her to give each of her realms in her spatial order its own room. In her apartment, her children's bedroom and playroom were in one room. In her new house, the children slept in an upstairs room and played downstairs in the television room next to her kitchen. Her previous kitchen had combined adult gatherings around the dining table with the second children's play area. In the new house, these two subareas went to separate rooms and her bedroom was placed in a room off the television room. The room with the bay window up front on the ground floor became her special living room, complete with her chairs and hi-fi, and further decorated by another new rug.

Just as in the Jung house, fully realizing a spatial order did not prevent further evolution of that order. In fact, full realization seemed to clear the air, enabling more subtle changes in Barbara's spatial order of home. She especially liked her new living room and began to elaborate on it. She now considered that it was really two spaces, joined face to face by an invisible seam (Figure 3-5). One half she considered as "lush, warm feeling with good light and rounded edges." This half was open to the street through a bay window, decorated in reds and blues, and plants and a round coffee table with a nice Oriental rug. The other half of the room she felt was "square-edged and modern," being decorated in browns and blacks with the stereo, sofa, and a chair. Her special space, the living room with its tea ritual, was further differentiating itself. Barbara was now a fuller and more complete woman of thirty-one years.

Like Barbara, Albert utilized rented apartments to continue his evolution of himself through his home spatial order. Albert was a twenty-seven-year-old engineer who had lived in suburban New Jersey with his wife. There they inhabited a one bedroom apartment. Their lives centered on the bedroom, where they ate their meals. Albert brought work home, which he did on the dining table. But he wanted to change his career and leave his suburban nine-to-five job. He re-entered graduate school and moved to Cambridge and the apartment pictured in Figure 3-6. In Cambridge, his household life shifted its focus from the bedroom to the living room. In his new private living room, he and his wife touched each other in new ways. Albert felt a part of a liberating new community. Instead of eating in the bedroom around the television or eating at the dining table, he and his wife drew the shades, sat naked on a pillow on the floor, and ate their meals with soft music playing on the hi-fi. For Albert, dining became a ritual that freed him from the confines of an old self.

Eating here at the dining table is very much like eating in a suburban-type environment. [But] we are very much interested in living the Cambridge existence. I like to be able to take advantage of certain freedoms that my apartment offers me. Last year, I wouldn't have felt comfortable sitting on the floor of my New Jersey apartment. Now we have a

FIGURE 3–5. Barbara's House

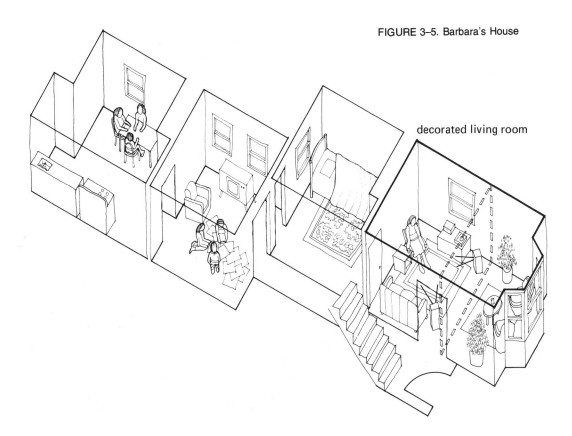

decorated living room

comfortable carpet . . . [and] I don't see any reason why we can't sit on the floor . . . I feel that I have transcended the confines of the table and chairs. It's one of my own small ways of saying I'm free.

Albert's new apartment also brought up his father's expectations for the son's career. In the new apartment, Albert finally had a separate study with a place for the desk his father had made for him. Albert saw that desk as his father's fantasy. Whereas the desk was big and bulky, Albert himself wished to be relaxed in his work. Whereas the desk was a practicing engineer's desk, Albert wanted a more dynamic, more deft career.

I don't like the desk. It is something my father made for me . . . It bites me. My father put that thing together with the idea of building me a big engineer's executive desk. Maybe last year I liked that idea, but as the thing started materializing, it appeared to me to be too heavy, too well constructed. I feel obligated to use it, although it affects my state of mind while I'm studying.

As we have seen in the spatial orders of Freud's young girl, home can powerfully define us by placing us in relationship to the people who live in the home with us. Albert's home spatial order provided him with an understanding of himself vis-à-vis his wife. They had both decorated their new apartment, assigning red, orange, and yellow rugs, prints, and furniture to the living room and study-guest room and blue and green rugs and furniture to the bedroom. To Albert, this color scheme manifested the differences between his wife and himself. Albert saw his wife as a subdued, cool, blue-green person. Those were her colors and her moods. The bedroom was where she used to hang out. The bedroom had the furniture that she had brought to their marriage. Albert saw himself as a more outward, effusive person, a red and orange fellow hanging out in the living and kitchen areas. Albert found a new ritual to cap off this elaboration of his home spatial order. Late at night, he would turn off the lights and light the candle he had placed inside a red and blue ship's beacon that hung in the hallway (Figure 3-6). He would then sit back in the living room and enjoy his apartment, now bathed in a special light. Red light spread out from the candle into the living room and the study. Blue light spread down the hall into the bedroom. He reflected on his new life. Red was space expressive of

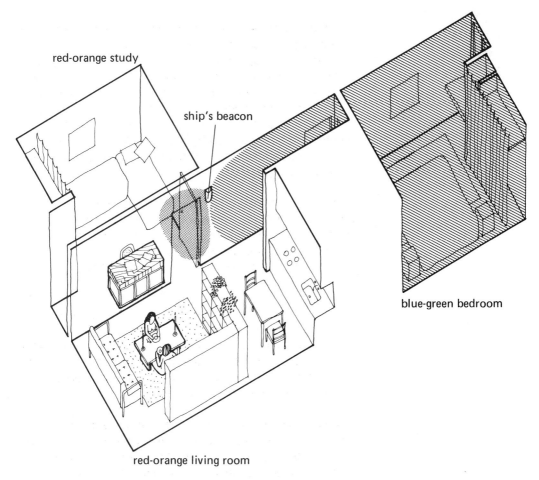

red-orange study

ship's beacon

blue-green bedroom

red-orange living room

FIGURE 3–6. Albert's Apartment

himself. Blue was space expressive of his wife. Red was the space of his waking hours. Blue was the space of his sleeping hours. In his apartment, Albert felt his way through a new career, a new lifestyle, and a new relationship with his wife.

Not all home spatial orders that define us vis-à-vis the people we live with are as seemingly neat and smooth as Albert's. Often, especially with younger families, home spatial orders are rough and conflicted as household occupants struggle with each other in the process of establishing a home.[6] Jill and Henry had moved as newlyweds into a

[6]For an accessible treatment see Glenn Lym, "Housing Urban Nomads," in *Residential Environments and the Family Life Cycle,* eds. Florence C. Ladd and Kathy Allott (Forthcoming). For a more thorough treatment see Lym, *Images of Home at Peabody Terrace* (unpublished doctoral dissertation, Harvard University, 1975), Chap. 5.

two room apartment. After three years they both wanted a larger place—yet each for different and conflicting reasons. Their conflicts focused on the extra room they acquired in a move to a new apartment. Jill saw her life as a highly entwined and intense collage of events and manipulations. She sought quiet for herself through meditation and through her home. In moving to their larger apartment, Jill wanted more room with which to separate the social situations of her household. To obtain this space, Jill ritually cleaned her apartment.

There is something sort of psychologically restful in having the place neat. It's never dusted nor shined. But when things are straightened out, it's one less chaotic thing to cope with. To come home after a chaotic day and have the apartment chaotic too does not ease the chaos.

In their new apartment (Figure 3-7), Jill wanted to separate the living room and the dining area by placing the latter in the extra new room they had acquired. But Henry, on the other hand, saw the new apartment as a chance to get a room all to himself. Henry intended to set up the extra room as his study and as a place in which he could make a mess by making his weekend clay pots.

We should each have a place that is all our own, that we can just do whatever we feel like, make all kinds of mess or noise. I'd have my pots all over. And when I would get done potting, I wouldn't clean up. It would be covered with shit on the floor.

Since Jill wanted the extra room to be a dining room, she insisted that the dining table go in it. Henry saw the table as a place to study or pot on as well as a place on which to eat. Jill wanted the extra room to be clean and nonchaotic, just like the rest of the apartment. She decorated the room with plants, a nice bedspread, a mat rug, a wicker basket, and a wooden lamp.

When it is cleaned up without dishes on the table or books being used, it's just very sunny, very light looking, very clean-cut.

Jill had given mess-loving Henry a clean-cut room. Henry quickly intuited the circumstances of this room. To him, this was "the sun room," a label that ambiguously reflected its

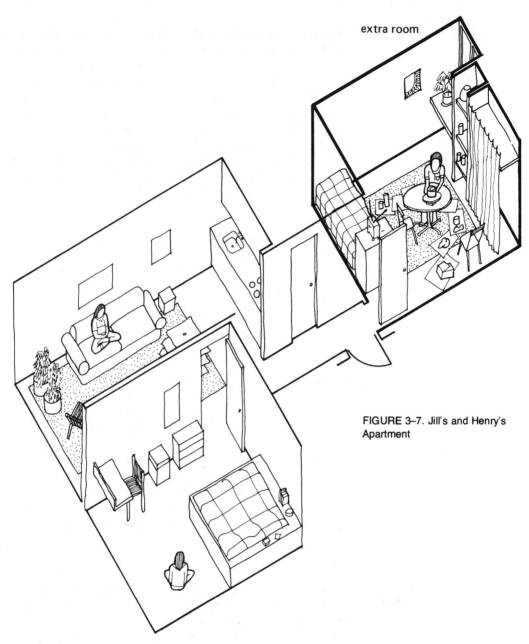

extra room

FIGURE 3–7. Jill's and Henry's Apartment

qualities as a sun-drenched room, as well as a place of struggle between himself as a son to a manipulatory wife-mother.

Jill and Henry were preparing to move to a new part of the country. Jill wanted an older home with many rooms so that she could continue to articulate and differentiate her household. She wanted a home that would realize her spatial order of separate places in which one household situation could not "get right on top of another." Henry was not at all concerned with articulated space. Instead, he wanted a country commune in which he and Jill would share their housing with several families, yet with everyone getting a special room to call their own. Henry envisioned a room where his mess would accumulate until he hosed it all down every so often. In the future, he was looking for housing that would realize his home spatial order of a room expressive of his own character set in the midst of an encompassing social structure.

For Schmidt, Jung, Barbara, Albert, Jill, and Henry, the evolution of a spatial order of home was an evolution of themselves. In his Woodstock home, Schmidt evolved an inclusive setting of internalized world orders. Jung evolved a geometric order of encircled maternal and spiritual towers with a central location between them. Barbara evolved an aggregate list of discrete home places. Albert evolved a color-coded, red-orange/blue-green home, contrasting yet uniting different aspects of his life and marriage. Jill evolved a spatial order of the home as clean, nonchaotic, and full of carefully separated places. And Henry evolved a spatial order of the home as a single personal place amid collective space. These evolving spatial orders became the vision by which these individuals evaluated and sought new housing. By seeking housing that would realize their spatial orders, these people entered into a responsive dialogue with their physical environments. That dialogue gave them insights about themselves and their lives. They used housing to reflect upon and to help come to terms with themselves.

the external order of the home

In our search for home, we give our interior home order an exterior context. This external order locates our home internal order in public space. This external order uses the public identities of nearby or conspicuously absent people further to delineate who we are. In an external order, we are selecting with whom we want to merge, against whom we want to set ourselves off, or who we want to avoid.

Schmidt made his home away from the bustling world that he had known in New York City all his life. He kept the world at a distance while he internalized the world's events and power within his home. Jung, too, was drawn to the countryside. Bollingen was set in a timeless place. At Bollingen, Jung felt himself connected to a great transpersonal past.

The place will outlive me . . . in its location and its style, it points backward to things of long ago. [7]

The home external order is important to our sense of ourselves. Perhaps the best way to illustrate this is by looking at the lives of those who have been denied a suitable location for their homes. The following is the tragic account of a man who was continually thwarted in his attempts to establish an external order for his home.

Earl L. Francis fled civilization two years ago. Recently, civilization caught up with him, ending his flight forever Tuesday. Mr. Francis, 33 years old, set out from Washington, D.C., for the wilds of Arizona in 1964, fed up with the variety of white-collar jobs he had held and the turmoil of 20th-century life. "I'll never work another eight-hour, six-day week for any man," he declared at the time. He selected a mile-high peak in the Catalina Mountains, overlooking Oracle, Arizona. During the next year, he worked day and night to build a cabin of stone and glass. . . . He settled back to read, paint, and meditate. But civilization was lurking nearby, in the form of the United States Forest Service. The site Mr. Francis had selected for his retreat from the world was part of the Coronado National Forest. The Forest Service informed Mr. Francis that he had to vacate his cabin since he was trespassing on public lands. Mr. Francis replied that he would never move. . . . Discouraged and expecting eviction, authorities reported, Mr. Francis sat down on a case of dynamite Tuesday, lit the fuse, and blew himself to pieces. [8]

In the early 1960s, social scientists and planners investigated an old Boston community called West End. West End was about to be destroyed, all its housing torn down to make way for upper middle class and upper class housing and parking. Mark Fried was one of the investigators. [9] He talked to West Enders before and after their eviction from

[7] Jung, *Memories*, pp. 231–232, 237.

[8] *New York Times*, August, 1966.

[9] Marc Fried, "Grieving for a Lost Home," in *The Urban Condition*, ed. Leonard Duhl (New York: Basic Books, 1963).

their homes and was struck by the grief reactions of these people. To West Enders, leaving their lifelong neighborhood and homes was equivalent to watching a close friend die. They grieved for the lost home and its place in West End.

Until the early 1970s, low-income housing complexes were subsidized by the federal government. Low-income families had no control over when and next to whom they would be housed within these complexes. One well-known complex in New Haven, Connecticut was designed by Charles Moore and William Turnbull. Its public pedestrian spaces were urbane and tightly crafted with minimal means. The individual units were designed as parodies of British urban town houses, complete with painted arch entrances, concrete block cornices and corner quoins (Figure 3-8). But to its black residents in 1975, the complex was an urban hell. One lady remarked, "It's a circus, honey. It tries to be something that it ain't." This woman and her neighbors lived in a dangerous ghetto, not in a sophisticated mid-urban village. She locked her door each night

FIGURE 3–8.
MLTW/Moore-Turnbull: Church Street South Housing, New Haven, Connecticut

Photo: Courtesy Marvin Buchanin

and forbade her daughter to leave the apartment after dark. Junkies lived next door. She feared for her own life and had tried to have bars installed over her windows. In the complex's picturesque "downtown" shopping area, vandals had demolished walls and smashed shop windows. Gaily painted signs and street furniture were broken. This woman and her neighbors aspired to middle class suburbia. She wanted to have a place of her own on land of its own away from junkies and other threats to her life.

Similar sentiments were voiced by residents of San Francisco low income housing projects during a series of group encounters with architects.[10] The residents saw their homes as a part of a large, alien complex. What seemed like an "urban community" to the architects was a "project" to the suburban-oriented residents. They drew their curtains day and night to secure their homes from prowlers and to shut out the presence of the "project." To them, their housing ruthlessly kept them in their place, away from the mainstream of American society. They experienced denial, both in achieving a place in society and in achieving an external order of home. To them, vandalism was a chronic space ritual destroying an unwanted external home order.

Most of us are lucky. In time we can realize the external order of our homes. As in the case of the internal order, we slowly evolve our external order as we grow and change in life. We achieve this external order in two different yet equally valid ways. We can experience community by face-to-face interaction. Being a part of a face-to-face community is to engage one's neighbors in a variety of public situations throughout the year. A fellow worker can be one's neighbor, one's minister, and the husband of one's cousin. A home set in a face-to-face community is situated in a community where one is known and knows others.[11] We can also experience community by reference contact. Reference community is community based on public masks and voyeuristic involvement with others. Actual contact

[10]Claire Cooper-Marcus, *Determination of Low-Income Resident Needs by Using Group Encounter Techniques* (unpublished report of the Housing Committee of the Northern California Chapter of the American Institute of Architects, James Weber director, 1969).

[11]A classic face-to-face definition of community is given in Jane Jacobs, *The Death and Life of Great American Cities* (New York: Random House, 1961), as well as Roger G. Barker and P. V. Gump, *Big School, Small School* (Palo Alto, Calif.: Stanford University Press, 1964).

between individuals is not required. In his sketch of the consumption community, historian Daniel Boorstin portrayed the essence of the reference community.

[*Such*] *a community consists of people who have a feeling of shared well-being, shared risks, common interests, and common concerns that come from consuming the same kinds of objects . . . The modern American is tied by the thinnest of threads . .. . to thousands of other Americans by nearly everything he eats or drinks or wears or reads or uses . . . We are held to other men not only by a few iron bonds, but by countless gossamer webs tying together the trivia of our lives every day.* [12]

Based as a reference community, the external order of the home focuses on public activity, dress, and places that suggest the community in which an individual wishes to be. Deviant characteristics of a locale are ignored.

In 1970 I encountered a young white man living in a pseudocommunity. We both lived in Riverside, a black community in Cambridge that dated back to the 1880s. Riverside had had an unusually well-knit, face-to-face community cross-tied by family, store, church, and children's activities destroyed by the expansion of local universities into the area. Small crime had increased, victimizing black and nonblack alike. My stereo was stolen, and I suspected that a young white man living down the back alley from me might have seen who did the deed. I knocked on his door. The young man answered. He refused to give me information, saying it was counterrevolutionary to turn blacks over to the white police state. The young man lived there with his revolutionary collective in a reference community. He told me that he lived in Riverside because it was "on the edge of society." He felt a part of the neighborhood because he offered dope to the local kids. He had never been invited into their homes or attended their gatherings. It was of no importance to him that most of the blacks in the neighborhood were working class people and aspired to middle-class American values of a new car, nice home decor, and good dress. He singled out and identified with their cynicism toward established white American society. Although he was not a member of their face-to-face com-

[12]Daniel J. Boorstin, "Welcome to the Consumption Community," *Fortune,* September 1, 1967, pp. 118–120.

munity, they provided him with the trappings of the reference community he needed to define himself as a political revolutionary.

Albert, too, located his apartment in a reference community. Although he knew no one who lived immediately near him, he felt a part of hip Cambridge and defined himself as such through his new activities such as nude dining.

There is a certain amount of osmosis that takes place here. People become, to whatever extent they are capable, a part of this whole community. And I have felt this happening to me. I'm trying to adjust my lifestyle to something I perceive is common around here.

Henry located his apartment in a reference community. In four-and-a-half years of living in a large apartment complex, he had never met the five or so other families with whom he shared an entryway. Henry saw his apartment as located adjacent to a reference community of hip, wooden apartment buildings and away from the sterile life of the tall, concrete towers at the center of his complex.

Phew! We're not in it, thank god. I think the towers are the center of ugliness . . . They are too grey and slablike. It's all economy and efficiency stuff. It's not nice and wooden.

In contrast, Jill based the external order of their home on both face-to-face and reference community experience. When she left her apartment, she felt she was not leaving the complex. Rather she thought of her apartment as located near Harvard Square, the reference community of shops and busy sidewalks that she visited on the weekends. Yet she was also a part of the face-to-face community of her housing complex. She spoke of entering her complex when she went to its little store where she was known by her first name and trusted.

Barbara based the external order of her home on both face-to-face and reference community experience. She had lived in an upper middle class Boston suburb, where she and her ex-husband had had a split-level home like all of her neighbors. Barbara felt uncomfortable there. She realized she had clothed herself in an inappropriate reference community. So she moved to Cambridge and to the apartment in Figure 3-4. There she more appropriately realized the external order of her home in another reference community. Now she was among a racially mixed population where there were real bread-and-butter political issues affecting working class families. This neighborhood had corner stores and turn-of-the-century houses and apartments in various states of repair and decay. All this appealed to Barbara's sense of being someone involved with real, human circumstances and human struggles. Later, she came to know and like the community as a face-to-face community. She liked participating in its food co-ops and community organizing and liked dealing with the diversity of neighbors and kids who dropped by her kitchen for coffee and play. Barbara felt very much at home. Her community had the just and unjust social involvement for which she was looking. This community gave her a sense of who she was in the outside world. Barbara made sure that her new house was one block away so it would maintain the external order she had come to like.

Taliesin   The story of Frank Lloyd Wright and the series of homes that he built for himself recalls Schmidt and his move from the city to the countryside. And like Jung's house, Wright's own houses were constantly being remodeled and added onto. Like Barbara, Albert, Earl Francis, and the low income dwellers, Wright's home underwent profound changes: divorces, new loves, deaths, burnings, and rebirths. However, examining the Wright homes is somewhat special. As with others in this chapter, we can see how an individual, faced with personal difficulties, created new home orders in response to his problems. But with Wright, his skill at or perhaps seriousness in addressing his problems helped him to create extraordinary architectural forms, anticipating home orders to come.

In 1890, a twenty-year-old Wright built a small house in the then fashionable classical-revival style (Figure 3-9). He located the house in the growing, upper middle class Chicago suburb of Oak Park and moved in with his seventeen-year-old bride. For almost twenty years, they raised a large family and were socially prominent in this bustling Victorian community. At the same time, Wright was at work creating a series of buildings to be known later as the Prairie Houses.

This was a period of great achievement for Wright, in which he struggled with architectural and social issues that would eventually fracture life in his own home. Norris Kelly Smith argued that Wright in this period was torn between two conceptions of the family.[13] He related to the family as a single, overall social entity with an interdependence among its members. Yet he considered the family as resulting from the actions taken by free individuals. During this period, Smith points out, Wright oscillated between two sorts of houses: houses of simple form (Figure 3-10) under a single wide roof, representing the family as a single social entity, and houses in which individual parts asserted their position, resulting in an irregular yet energized ensemble (Figure 3-11). In some of his early houses, a single house would embody both of these formal aspects. The front of a house might be a singular mass, while the rear erupted into multiple forms sliding up and past each other.

FIGURE 3–9. Frank Lloyd Wright: First Wright House, Oak Park, Illinois

Photo: H. R. Hitchcock

[13]Norris Kelly Smith, *Frank Lloyd Wright: A Study in Architectural Content* (Englewood Cliffs, N.J.: Prentice-Hall, Inc., 1966), pp. 60–61.

FIGURE 3–10. (*above*). Frank Lloyd
Wright: Heurtley House, Oak Park,
Illinois

Photo: H. R. Hitchcock

FIGURE 3–11 (*below*). Frank Lloyd
Wright: House, Oak Park, Illinois

Photo: Murray Silverstein

Toward the end of this period, Wright resolved this conflict. He came to see that buildings should be formed from their insides outward. Just as the person of integrity and conviction derives strength and actions from within rather than from external social mores, so too would the Prairie Houses be formed from within. Further, people were no longer to live boxed up in Victorian homes. The Prairie House allowed space and movement to flow freely through the house. Wright stressed freedom of horizontal movement on the land, for the people of the American midwest plains. These became a part of the internal order of the Prairie Houses.

Wright was unable to achieve a cohesive whole out of a free play of individual spaces in his own house. He continually remodeled his house, adding among other places, a barrel-vaulted playroom for his children and a studio for his architectural practice (Figure 3-12). His favorite spot was by a fireplace in his study, tucked halfway between his house and his office. But life within the house seemed to sap his freedom. In 1909 at the height of his success, Wright abandoned his office, his social life, and his family—an unheard of scandal for that era. He wrote:

Everything, personal or otherwise, bore heavily down upon me. Domesticity most of all . . . What I wanted I did

FIGURE 3–12. Frank Lloyd Wright: Additions to First Wright House, Oak Park, Illinois

Photo: Murray Silverstein

not know. I loved my children. I loved my home. A true home is the finest ideal of man, and yet—well, to gain freedom I asked for a divorce.[14]

Over the next twenty-five years, Wright sought to realize the internal order of the Prairie Houses in houses for himself, sited by a new and evolving external order. He went to Europe for a passionate and wonderful year with the wife of a client. Upon his return, he took up residence in rural Wisconsin. Rather than return to the regimentation of the upper middle class communities, Chicago and Oak Park, Wright chose to settle in the countryside that he identified with his ancestors. At Taliesin, the Prairie House would grow from the earth just as Wright intended to be reborn from the soil of his ancestors.

I turned to this hill in the Valley as my Grandfather before me had turned to America—as a hope and haven . . . Now I wanted a natural house to live in myself. I scanned the hills of the region where the rock came cropping out in strata to suggest buildings . . . Yes, there was a house that hill might marry and live happily with ever after . . . And I began to build it as the brow of that hill.[15]

The result of Wright's efforts was Taliesin (Figure 3-13), the home he made for the woman with whom he then lived. At Taliesin, he would build a new family. He had taken his home from its oppressive face-to-face community in the city and placed it in a reference community in which he had felt free to grow as an individual. He had created for himself a home whose space, forms, material, and site were congruent with his evolving spatial order for the home. Smith wrote

Taliesin was a rich and subtle embodiment of an idea of which Wright had achieved at best only a partial and inadequate expression heretofore—the idea of a spacious, rambling symbol of the family, rooted not in the arbitrary grid of the city but in Nature herself.[16]

But if Taliesin was an architectural success, it was yet to be the home Wright sought. In 1914, Taliesin burned down,

[14]Frank Lloyd Wright, *An Autobiography* (New York: Horizon Press, 1943, 1977), p. 187.

[15]Ibid., pp. 167–169.

[16]Smith, *Frank Lloyd Wright,* p. 106.

killing his lover. Wright was devastated. Chicago public opinion considered the tragedy to be Wright's punishment for leading a scandalous life. Bereaved, he rebuilt Taliesin, but he did not spend much time there over the next twelve years. He traveled to Japan and to the western United States working on new commissions.

In 1925, Taliesin II also burned. But now, in his fifties, Wright rebuilt Taliesin out of the ashes and laid the foundations for the home and community for which he had longed. Taliesin III became the home of a wonderful new marriage to Olgivanna, which would last until his death some thirty years later. Olgivanna persuaded Wright to set up an apprentice community at Taliesin. Life in the new Taliesin Fellowship came to include office practice, building, farming, music, dancing, and weekend talks by Wright and visiting celebrities.

In the Prairie Houses, Wright had synthesized the internal order of the home he himself had sought but not found. In Taliesin I, he built himself that internal order and began to bring to it its pseudocommunity external order, its location on the open land. But it was not until Taliesin III that Wright was fully at home. There he realized both the internal and external order of his home. Wright now had a base from which he would produce yet another generation of buildings in the 1930s, the Usonian houses.

FIGURE 3–13. Frank Lloyd Wright: Taliesin I, Spring Green, Wisconsin
Photo: Fuermann

FIGURE 3–14 (*above*) and 3–15 (*below*). Building a Home in New Hampshire

Photos: Glenn Lym and Floyd Tomkins

So far, we have seen some homes under construction and some homes blown up or burned to the ground. The home, like the life it models, grows and decays. In seeking home, we bring our lives into a dialogue with our physical environment. We may create rigidifying or open and expansive home spatial orders. We may ingest the greater world or exclude it and reflect upon inner experiences. We may evolve ourselves in rented housing or build a house to custom-fit our spatial orders. We may actively include or exclude the people we live with in our spatial orders. We may struggle for our internal order of home. In realizing our spatial order of home, we are embarked upon a lifelong, continuing journey. In seeking home and its location on earth, we spatialize our lives. We become architects for our homes and architects of our lives.

being our own architects

4

**professional
building**

personal expression and the architect

This chapter makes a deceptively simple point. The art of professional building, like lay building, is based upon making spatial orders manifest. For architects, as for lay persons, building is the creation of a spatial order for an institution and the subsequent manifestation of that spatial order as a building.

This point is deceptive because all current indications are that what is wrong with professional building is precisely that it does not employ the same design processes that lay people naturally use. At present, lay people, design people, and social scientists feel that professional designers see space in a fundamentally different way than nondesigners. It is this fundamental difference that critics point to as the basis for architecture's apparent failure to meet the needs of clients and building users.

The origin of this viewpoint is easy to see. Architects, urban planners, and landscape architects emphasize the formal spatial and visual aspects of their work. They may often express little interest in the relationship of these formal spatial devices to the lives of their clients and users. Often at great personal sacrifice, designers may spend years developing and refining these formal devices. Architect I.M. Pei and his staff developed innovative ways to create and shape concrete. Pei developed intricate casting procedures so that a research center in Colorado would appear as a single piece of concrete unblemished by variations in color and texture, as the concrete was poured successively floor by floor. Pei wanted the building to stand as a single object against the majestic Rocky Mountains. Frank Lloyd Wright built structures in which planes of wood bent and wobbled if you pushed against them, yet they supported the roof. He built wooden floors with air spaces between the planks through which heat could rise. When you walked on these floors, the soles of your shoes bounced on the planks. Wright wanted to use wood in a way that reflected both its flexibility and its strength.

The geometry of a building's exterior facade can be a major formal device for architects. In 1966, Robert Venturi published his early thoughts on architecture[1] and discussed his design for a YMCA in Ohio (Figure 4-1). He talked of the

[1]Robert Venturi, *Complexity and Contradiction in Architecture* (New York: Museum of Modern Art, 1966).

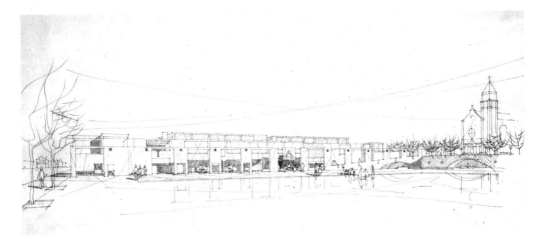

visual syncopation of the openings of his building's two-dimensional, free-standing wall against the three-dimensional form of the building beyond. He was excited by the way in which the free-standing wall "fronted" for the more amorphous portion of the building behind.

FIGURE 4–1. Venturi and Rauch: Y.M.C.A., Canton, Ohio

Strongly phrased statements and designs for a purely formal architecture have come from Peter Eisenman, who sought to create an architecture of its own internal meaning devoid of any traditional or user meanings. His House III could be understood as having begun with a simple cubic space (Figure 4-2a). This cube was then divided by vertical planes (Figure 4-2b). Then it was rotated in relation to the planes (Figure 4-2c). These planes were then sheared and displaced with respect to each other (Figure 4-2d). Further transformations revealed the final design (Figure 4-3).

Eisenman wrote

Because of the way the formal structure seems to influence an individual, its expression reduces or takes away known meaning [of the house] . . . This expression of the formal system produces an architecture divested of traditional meaning . . . it excludes the design of those things which, through design, reinforce traditional meaning, such as interior finishes, the location and style of furniture, or the installation of lighting . . . In this sense, when the owner first enters "his house" he is an intruder; he must begin to regain possession—to occupy a foreign container . . .[2]

[2]Peter Eisenman, and others, "House III," *Progressive Architecture* (May 1974), p. 92.

Given professional designers' intense interest in the formal aspects of architecture, it is little wonder that they have come under criticism by people concerned with the living quality of the everyday environment. Social scientists argue that designers must shift their attention from formal, visual concerns and consider building users. Social scientist Terence Lee wrote

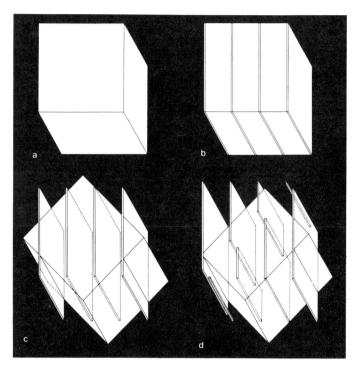

FIGURE 4–2 (a to d). Peter Eisenman: Studies for House III

[*My work*] *is an appeal* [*to the architect*] *to forsake the traditional . . . form of architectural service. This was to cater, first and foremost for only one of man's needs—the visual aesthetic; to put above all things the emotional impact of buildings and to measure this impact on an elite of spectators* [*other design professionals*] *whose overt behavior is not affected nor shaped by the building at all.*[3]

Environmental psychologist Robert Sommer concurred, calling on the architect to pay less attention to "personal expression" and more attention to the people and functions served by buildings.

[3]Terence Lee, "The Psychology of Spatial Orientation," *Architectural Association Quarterly* (1970), 1:14.

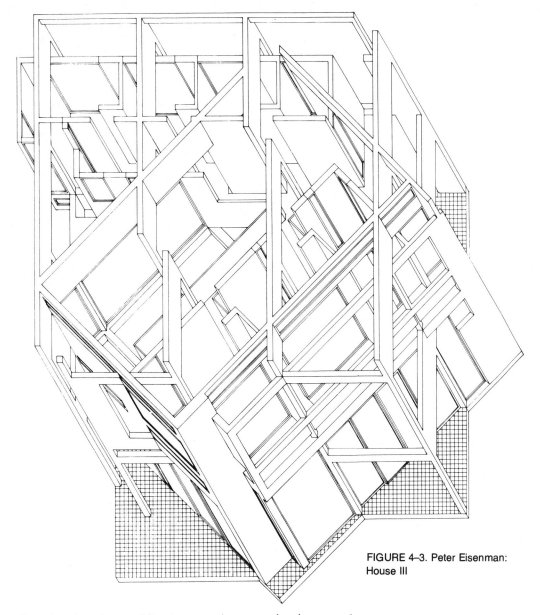

FIGURE 4–3. Peter Eisenman: House III

The doctrine that architecture can be conceived as great hollow sculpture or timeless, unchanging form whose existence is an end in itself must be discarded. Not only must form follow function, but it must assist it in every way. The personal expression of the architect must yield to the functions that the building serves.[4]

[4]Robert Sommer, *Personal Space* (Englewood Cliffs, N.J.: Prentice-Hall, Inc., 1969), pp. 4–5.

But this viewpoint that professional and lay people experience space and build in fundamentally different ways is incorrect. From earlier chapters, we know that lay people themselves do not put aside their "personal expression" and build merely to solve functional issues. In their criticisms of designers, Lee and Sommer could also have been criticizing lay people as well. We know that lay people intuitively see important life issues spatially. Schmidt's power images, Jung's tower forms, and Albert's apartment color décor (discussed in Chapter Three) were themselves architectural formalisms attending to deep personal and social issues. It is clear that attention to the formal properties of architecture is not in itself a mark of insensitivity to "user needs" or to users' lives.

If we want to evaluate professional building, we must first examine the spatial orders that motivate a good designer's work. We can do this through an examination of the works of Eero Saarinen, Le Corbusier, Frank Lloyd Wright, and Louis Kahn. Then we shall be in a position to understand properly that good professional building is dependent upon a special interaction between the spatial orders of the designer and the client-user and not upon a forfeiting of the "personal expression" of either the designer or the client-user.

the spatial orders of professional designers

In good design, architects use their formal devices to realize spatial orders that they feel are important to their users. Like lay builders, professional designers intuitively want to nurture the chronic space experience of the people who will use their buildings. And like lay people, designers do this by formulating spatial orders that structure their designs. For designers, just as for lay people, the aim of building is to create space that effectively folds into the life of its occupants.

We begin with Eero Saarinen, an architect who came close to seeing, but did not quite see, design as the creator of spatial order for clients. He wanted the formal devices of his buildings to have relevance to his users. In his late commissions, his office brilliantly devised new formal devices— new building materials and forms—to express the "character" of his clients. For the John Deere Company headquarters building in Moline, Illinois, Saarinen wanted a rugged steel building in character with the farm machinery made by

Deere. So his office pioneered in the use of an exposed, rust-protected, brown structure steel (Figure 4-4). Saarinen commented

FIGURE 4–4. Eero Saarinen and Associates: John Deere Building, Moline, Illinois

Photo: John Deere Co.

Farm machinery is not slick, shiny metal but forged iron and steel in big, forceful, functional shapes. The proper character for its headquarters' architecture should likewise not be a slick, precise, glittering glass and spindly metal building, but a building which is bold and direct, using metal in a strong, basic way. [5]

Saarinen's designs usually did not penetrate deeply into the nature of his client-users. His design process did not acknowledge the acute and chronic space experience of his buildings' users. He designed for the largely tangential, surface characteristics of those users. And thus, Saarinen wanted an exposed steel, forceful office building for the maker of large iron farm equipment.

But architecture goes beyond expressing the surface character of its client-users. Architecture can become meaning. For this to happen, architects search directly for important space experiences that a user might have in their buildings. To do this, architects must identify the life issues of the users and anticipate the objects, space, and rituals related to those issues. The result of this kind of analysis is something that designers call a "design concept." And a design concept is really another term for what we have called in this book a "spatial order." A design concept or spatial order is a set of spatial conditions that architects feel will create, as well as preserve, the user's important chronic space experience. Clearly great skill is required for architects to do such an analysis. Yet it has been done many times throughout the history of architecture.

In the early 1950s, the famous French-Swiss architect Le Corbusier designed a monastery in rural Eveux, France. His client asked him to familiarize himself with the austere, medieval Cistercian monasteries. Corbusier was inspired by the beauty and simplicity of these works. In his own monastery, Corbusier created simple yet texturally rich interior and exterior surfaces out of bare concrete and rugged white stucco. Like Saarinen's pioneering formal devices, these textures had tremendous impact upon international architecture, inspiring what became known as the new brutalist style. But unlike Saarinen, Corbusier's search for the essence of his commission did not stop here. He was not just interested in capturing a monastery's simplicity in a

[5]Eero Saarinen, *Eero Saarinen on His Works* (New Haven, Conn.: Yale University Press, 1962), p. 76.

new architectural surface treatment. His invention of a new textural surface was just a by-product of a deeper search, a search for the spatial order of a monastery.

Le Corbusier was fascinated by the organization of the Cistercian monasteries, where the refectory, the dormitories, the chapel, and other elements were plugged into a four-square cloister walkway, which in turn encircled an open-air court. The monks would walk this cloister, meditating on and encircling the central void. At Eveux, Le Corbusier had a steep hillside site. He decided to order his monastery from the top down. It would encircle a central void with concrete passage and stair tubes criss-crossing the void at midair (Figure 4-5). The cloister walk would now be on the rooftops of the encircling buildings. Le Corbusier passionately anticipated a monk's chronic space experience of walking on the rooftop cloister.

FIGURE 4–5. Le Corbusier: Convent of Saint Mary of La Tourette, Eveux, France, with Rooftop Cloister

Photo: J. Cellard from *Oeuvre Complète,* Vol. 7, Verlag fur Architecktur Artemis, Zurich

There was a moment when the idea came to me: put the cloister there—high up. But if I put it up there it will be so beautiful the monks may make it a distraction which might endanger their religious life, because it will create an uncertainty in their magnificent, courageous life. They have a difficult interior life which is very strong. The delights of sky and clouds are at times too easy. Let them go there from time to time, let someone authorize them to climb the stairs to the roof; it's an outing for those who have shown prudence . . . Thus you have a building, very precise at the top, and which, by degrees, organizes itself as it descends and touches the ground as it can. This is something which is . . . unique to this convent, very original.[6]

In Frank Lloyd Wright's 1906 design for a Unitarian church in Oak Park, Illinois, Wright began just as Le Corbusier did, by seeking a spatial order for his clients. Unity Temple was one of the first public structures in the United States to be built of reinforced concrete. Yet this innovative formal device was incidental to Wright's search for a vision that would realize the chronic space of his church. He found it in the spatial order of a meeting place not aspiring to the heavens but rooted in the ground. He wrote

Why not . . . build a temple, not to God . . . but build a temple to man, appropriate to his uses as a meeting place, in which to study man himself for his God's sake.[7]

To design Unity Temple, Wright explored in detail the formal devices implied by the spatial order of the church as a meeting room. A meeting room should be quiet. So he placed its entrance away from the noisy intersection outside. He wanted the room to be skylit with amber glass so that, regardless of weather, it would always be bathed in warm light, (Figure 4-6). Wright carefully considered how people would meet in the room. The congregation was to be seated in the cubic volume with overlooking side balconies. It was a space focused on the pulpit, yet open and responsive to the calls from the seated congregation. People entered from passageways a half-story below the room so that they would not disturb the dignity and quiet. And when

[6]Le Corbusier, "Entretien avec Le Corbusier," *L'Art Sacré* (March-April 1960), pp. 7–9. Excerpt translated by Linda Weingarten.

[7]Frank Lloyd Wright, *An Autobiography* (New York: Horizon Press, 1943, 1977), pp. 177–178.

they left, people did not turn their backs on the pastor. Rather, they came forward and passed by either side of the pulpit and down stairs through swinging doors directly into the entrance loggia. Like Le Corbusier, Wright's formal design devices, such as these lighting and circulation patterns, were at the service of the spatial order of Unity Temple as a meeting room.

Most of Wright's commissions were residential. In these designs, he sought the spatial order of home. As we discussed in Chapter Three, Wright developed a spatial order that became known as the Prairie House. For him, home and human were one. As people had moral integrity, so should their homes have integrity. As human integrity was an inner quality that shaped the person, so should the home have an inner quality shaping its exterior. As integrity was also a matter of the continuity of a person's ideals and actions, so should the parts of a home be constructed of materials flowing into each other as a continuous, integral

FIGURE 4–6. Frank Lloyd Wright: Unity Church, Oak Park, Illinois
Photo: Fuermann

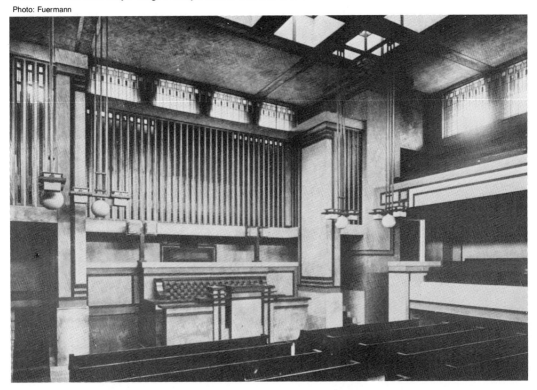

whole. And as integrity implied freedom for the individual, so should the home have a new spatial freedom (Figure 4-7). The Prairie House abandoned the boxiness of late Victorian and Classical Revival houses typical of that period. A fireplace was at the core of the Prairie House. Its spaces grew from inside out. Walls, ceilings, and floors were tied to each other, yet flowed past each other as integral parts of a whole. The house felt like a shelter protected under wide roofs with vistas out onto the landscape and a fireplace within. These were revolutionary architec-

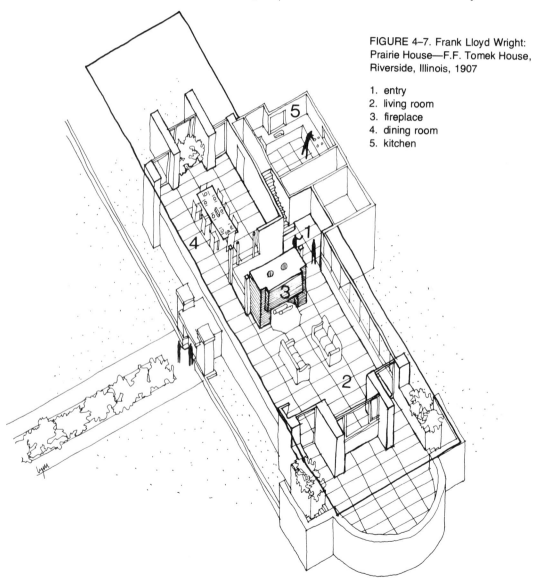

FIGURE 4–7. Frank Lloyd Wright: Prairie House—F.F. Tomek House, Riverside, Illinois, 1907

1. entry
2. living room
3. fireplace
4. dining room
5. kitchen

tural devices that Wright had created to realize a new spatial order for a new kind of American family.

Twenty years later, America was in the Depression. Wright refined his spatial order for the American home. The building program of parlor, library, and loggias gave way to the simple two- and three-bedroom house with a kitchenette. Using new but austere formal design devices, he reinterpreted the spatial order of the Prairie House and created the Usonian House (Figure 4-8). The Usonian House began

FIGURE 4–8. Frank Lloyd Wright: Usonian House—Herbert Jacobs House I, Madison, Wisconsin, 1937

1. entry
2. living room
3. fireplace
4. dining room
5. kitchen

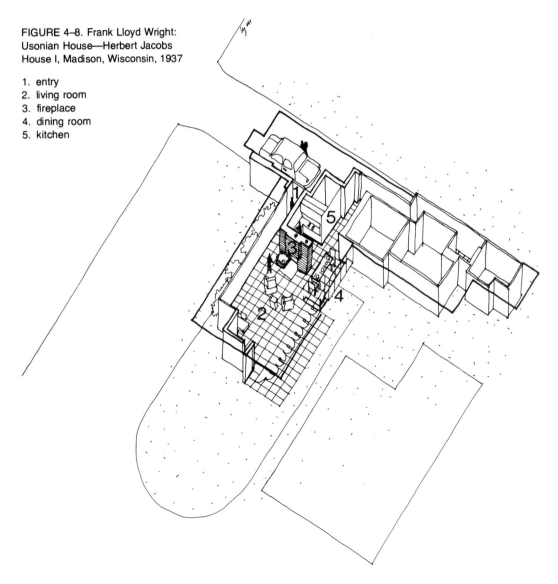

as a simple home that in its austerity had fierce integrity. Retaining many of the principles of the Prairie House, such as inner integrity, continuity, and horizontal freedom, the Usonian House began as a simple concrete slab poured on the earth and embedded with coils for radiant heating. Walls were of brick or cypress inside and out, using a new material—plywood—sandwiched in between. Roofs were supported by laminated two-by-fours. The resultant interiors required no decoration, painting, or trim. The heart of the new home became a masonry fireplace—kitchen open to a dining alcove.

The Usonian House . . . aims to be a natural performance, one that is integral to site, integral to environment, integral to the life of the inhabitants, a house integral with the nature of material—wherein glass is used as glass, stone as stone, wood as wood.[8]

Wright also developed an explicit, external order for the Usonian House. It was to be located in Wright's ideal of a regional democracy that he called Usonia. Wright found the dense twentieth-century city ill-proportioned and oppressive to self-willed, free people. The city was a social evil that had to be countered by decentralization. Just as the new interior spaciousness of the Prairie and Usonian Houses was to free the individual, Wright felt that ending urban centralization and allowing individuals free horizontal movement on the land would realize a free American democracy.

So Wright proposed the spatial order of Broadacre City. In models and in illustrations, years before the development of America's post World War II suburbs, Wright proposed a city based on mobility and centered on the individual in his or her Usonian House rooted on the earth. At birth, everyone was to receive an acre of land to build on and cultivate. Business, government, shopping, manufacturing, and church sites were to be dispersed in and among farms, forests, lakes, and houses. People were to get about in quiet electric cars traveling on widely spaced highways. To build Broadacre would be to realize nothing less than Usonian democracy.

[8]Frank Lloyd Wright, *The Natural House* (New York: New American Library, Mentor Books, 1954), p. 123.

Think of the immense advantages for your children and for yourself: freedom to use the ground, relationship with all kinds of living growth . . . The only answer to life today is to get back to the good ground . . . Not the city going to the country but the country and city becoming one.[9]

When democracy builds, this is the natural city of freedom in space . . . the nature of democracy when actually built.[10]

Like Wright, architect Louis I. Kahn also understood design as the creation of spatial orders by which to realize social institutions. Kahn stated

Every architect's first act is that of either revitalizing a prevailing belief or finding a new belief which is just in the air somehow.[11]

The door is open, very open to the realization of wonderful new institutions.[12]

Kahn sought what he termed the "beginning."

For a commission in the 1960s to design the Indian Institute of Management in Ahmedabad, India, Kahn sought the beginnings of "school." He wanted to know the archetypal nature of "school," what its energy and spirit were. To design this school meant to create a spatial order for the Institute, yet one firmly rooted in the original intentions of "school." Kahn stated

Schools began with a man under a tree, a man who did not know he was a teacher, discussing his realizations with a few others who did not know they were students. The students reflected on the exchanges between them and on how good it was to be in the presence of this man. They wished their sons, also, to listen to this man. Soon the needed spaces were erected and the first schools came into existence . . . Our vast systems of education, now

[9]Wright, *Natural House,* p. 135.

[10]Frank Lloyd Wright, *The Living City* (New York: New American Library, Mentor Books, 1958), p. 120.

[11]Louis I. Kahn, "Remarks," *Perspecta: The Yale Architecture Journal,* 9-10:305 (1965).

[12]Louis I. Kahn, "Louis Kahn: Statements on Architecture," *Zodiac,* 17:57 (1967).

vested in institutions, stem from these little schools, but the spirit of their beginning is now forgotten. The rooms required by our institutions of learning are stereotyped and uninspiring . . . Such schools, though good to look at, are shallow as architecture, because they do not reflect the spirit of the man under the tree.[13]

Kahn searched endlessly for formal devices to realize his spatial order of school as an inspired meeting place. How were teacher and student to be together? Are they together in the same way in an intimate room with a fireplace as in a large room? Instead of seminar rooms, why not talk of places of inspiration? Why not consider the cafeteria for the learning that takes place there across a relaxed meal? Why not consider the corridor that connects classrooms as a gallery where students can talk among themselves about what was not understood within? From questions such as these, Kahn designed the Institute with classrooms having vestibules between them that spilled onto a long gallery with more vestibules and openings (Figure 4-9). There were stairs that went up to the classroom roofs where classes could be held in the open air if the weather permitted. The landings of these stairs, the gallery itself, and the vestibules were all places for in between class encounters. Kahn placed the library between the classrooms and the faculty offices as yet another area for faculty student encounter. The student quarters were immediately adjacent to the classrooms so that living and learning could be one.

When asked to design a theater in Indiana, Kahn sought the beginning of "theater." He came to understand "theater" as a collection of places all focused on the stage as a plaza. There was the auditorium where the audience could become entranced with the presentation and with itself (Figure 4-10).

I thought further of the meaning of a place of assembly like a Philharmonic Hall . . . you would say that the music is only partly important; décolleté is important; seeing a person and becoming entranced is also important . . . seeing the entire hall—not to be forced by its shape to look at it from under a balcony, not just to hear music, but to feel the entire

[13]Louis I. Kahn, *The Notebooks and Drawings of Louis I. Kahn*, eds. Richard S. Wurman and Eugene Feldman (Cambridge, Mass.: M.I.T. Press, 1974), p. 71.

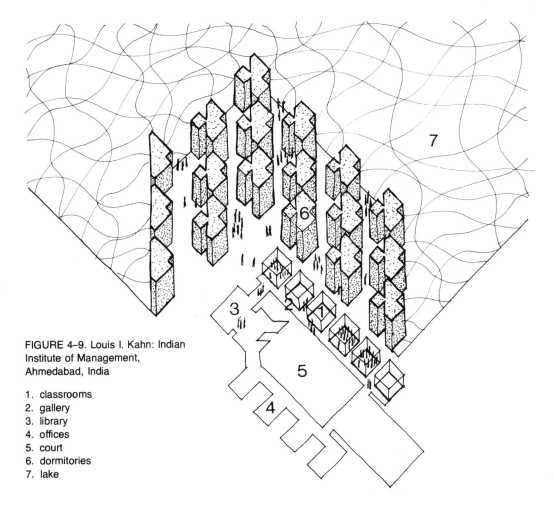

FIGURE 4–9. Louis I. Kahn: Indian
Institute of Management,
Ahmedabad, India

1. classrooms
2. gallery
3. library
4. offices
5. court
6. dormitories
7. lake

*chamber—because being in the chamber is like living in
the violin. The chamber itself is an instrument. If you think a
great deal about such a place, you can come to the realization that in the design of a theater, you are making a musical
instrument containing people.*[14]

There were spaces for the actors to rehearse and shape
their art. He thought of a place for the actors to become
themselves before belonging to the play. This would be the
actors' chapel. The actors' spaces were the sacred spaces
of the theater. Their spaces would constitute an actor's
house with its own porch overlooking the stage. And the
stage itself was a plaza in which actors and audience met in
the guise of a performance.

[14]Kahn, "Remarks," p. 318.

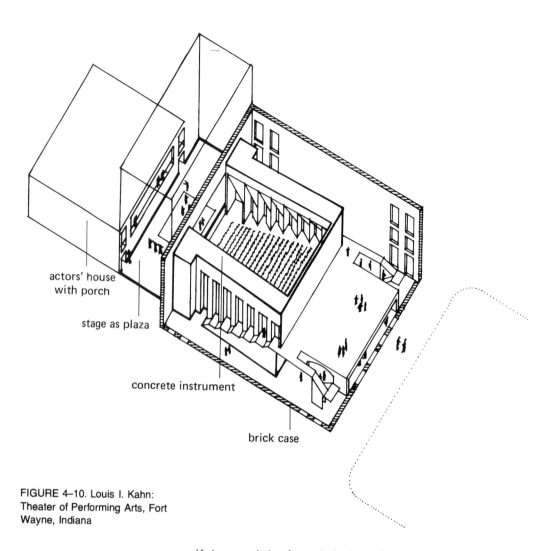

actors' house
with porch

stage as plaza

concrete instrument

brick case

FIGURE 4–10. Louis I. Kahn:
Theater of Performing Arts, Fort
Wayne, Indiana

Kahn used the formal device of contrasting architectural
materials to build his spatial order of the theater. He designed the audience-instrument as a folded concrete box,
which he placed inside a larger, contrasting brick box—the
"violin case" as he called it (Figure 4-10). The space between the brick case and the concrete instrument became
the lounges and lobbies for the audience. At the beginning
of a performance, the audience entered the brick box and
then the concrete box and was seated. The musicians and
actors were in their house, ready to descend to the stage.
When the curtain rose, all these people became participants in a drama set in a public meeting place, the stage as
a plaza.

Le Corbusier, Wright, and Kahn knew chronic space. They realized that to manipulate space was to manipulate the chronic space experiences of a building's users. So they examined the chronic space experiences of their users in order to formulate spatial orders for those users and their social institutions.

The work of Le Corbusier, Wright, and Kahn included generous attention to the formal devices of design. Yet their interests in material combinations and building forms and spaces were simply means by which spatial orders were transformed into built form. Contrary to Lee and Sommer's criticisms, these architects were merely doing what lay people do all the time when being their own architects. These architects understood design as the realization of spatial orders.

So we know that design by spatial orders is a task undertaken by lay people and by professional designers alike. We need not see designers as bizarre people intent on self-indulgence at the expense of their users. Professional and lay building follows the same human process, chronic space experience inspiring a spatial order that becomes the vision that guides building.

the problematic relationship of professional and users' spatial orders

But is there not a problem in the relationship of professional design spatial orders to the spatial orders of the users? Do bad environments result if designers' and users' spatial orders do not match?

There is an assumption, in questions such as these, that building properly is a matter of anticipating correctly the chronic space experience of the users. From this perspective, designers simply function as extensions of the users. This assumption is operationally incorrect. Buildings that realize a designer's spatial order do not directly impose that order upon occupants. As we saw with the apartment dwellers in Chapter Three, occupants come into a pre-designed space and impose their own spatial order upon the building. The worst a professional building can do is interfere with its users' imposition of their own spatial orders. Consider House III, which architect Eisenman designed purposely ignoring his clients' own spatial orders (Figure 4-3). Eisenman wanted a building not generated by what he termed "traditional meanings." He spoke of the owner as "an intruder" who had to "regain possession" of his home when he first moved into it. Yet the owner's account of House III was not the lament of a tired conqueror. The owner loved the house because he could install his own spatial order in it. The owner wrote

Our concept from the start was to build a modern version of a Mykonos house. And that's the way we've furnished it: with country peasant furniture . . . We've filled it with Moroccan rugs, French country tables, clay pots filled with geraniums, hanging plants, an antique Austrian chest, etc. [Figure 4-11]. And to our taste, it works perfectly.[15]

The owner's dissatisfactions were not with struggles he had against the house as a foreign space. Rather, his dissatisfaction came from a few aspects of the house that distracted him from his spatial order of a secure, Greek Island home—namely a leaky roof and poor summer ventilation.

The assumption that designers function as extensions of their users is also strategically incorrect. Although a building that realizes a designer's spatial order does not directly impose that order on a user, that order can subtly enhance the user's chronic space experience. When a designer has properly formulated a spatial order, the resultant building can work with the users' own spatial orders and deepen those users' spatial experience. The building has its own wisdom to impart to its users, so to speak. Such a building is Louis Kahn's library at the preparatory academy in Exeter, New Hampshire.

Unlike House III, the Exeter Library derived from a meticulously crafted spatial order that tried to anticipate its users' own chronic space experience. Kahn had given much thought to libraries before he received this commission. Almost a decade before the Exeter commission, Kahn had come to the conclusion that the basic chronic space of "library" was the individual inspired by a book. Reading a book was a ritual that inspired the reader. To read in a library was to bring a book from a dark, protective shelf into sunlight. This sunlight celebrated the reader's illumination by the book. Sunlight would be at the periphery coming into

[15]Eisenman, "House III," p. 98.

the building between columns. There between the columns were the carrels where person and book encountered each other.

FIGURE 4–11. Peter Eisenman: House III
Photo: Martin Tornallyay

A man with a book goes to the light. A library begins that way. The carrel is the niche which could be the beginning of the space order and its structure. The reading room is impersonal. It is the meeting in silence of the readers and their books.[16]

Several years later, Kahn talked of another way in which people might be inspired by books in a library. There would be places in which wonderful books would be laid open, there to entice passers-by.

Now if you had a library where you just had broad tables . . . upon which books lie and these books are open . . . They are planned very, very cleverly by the librarian to open at pages that humiliate you with the marvelous drawings . . . If a teacher could make comment on these books, so a seminar is spontaneous, this would be marvelous.[17]

At Exeter, Kahn provided for both these rituals in an intricate donut spatial order (Figure 4-12). He outlined this order to architectural critic Bill Marlin.

Exeter begins with the periphery where the light is. I felt the reading room would be where a person is alone near a window, and I felt that would be a private carrel, a kind of discovered place in the folds of construction [Figure 4-13]. I made the outer depth of the building like a brick donut, independent of the books. I made the inner depth of the building like a concrete donut where the books are stored away from the light. The center area is a result of these two contiguous donuts. It's just the entrance where the books are all visible all around you through the big circular openings so you feel that the building has the invitation of books [Figure 4-14].[18]

Around that central area, Kahn placed wooden, display shelves for open books—say to a map of an ancient land or to a page from the *Whole Earth Catalogue*. Outside, the

[16]Louis I. Kahn, "Statements" (remarks transcribed by Patrick Quinn at the University of California, Berkeley, 1960).

[17]Louis I. Kahn, "Louis I. Kahn: Talks with Students," *Architecture at Rice* (Houston, Tex.: Rice University), 26:42–43.

[18]William Marlin, ed., "The Mind of Louis Kahn," *Architectural Forum*, 137:1 (July-August 1972), 77.

library was a brick cube, hinting of the layering of brick and concrete within (Figure 4-15). At Exeter, at the heart of this brick cube was the cubic void of the central area.

In the spring of 1975, I spent several days at the Exeter Library and interviewed eighteen of its teenaged users. My first impression was that what Exeter users found in the

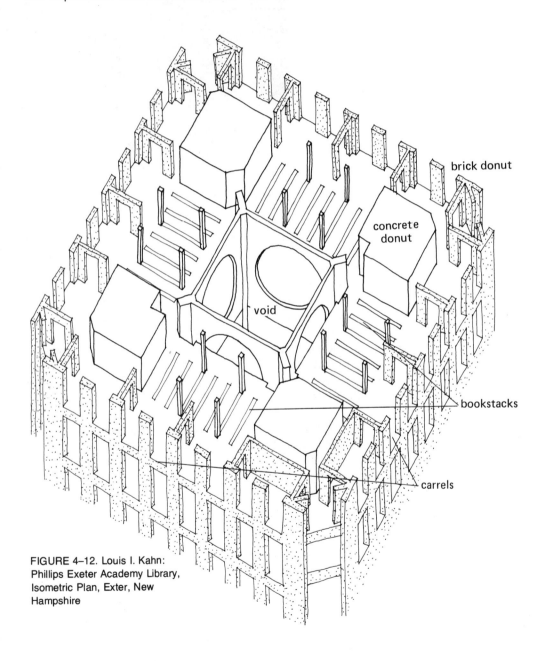

FIGURE 4–12. Louis I. Kahn: Phillips Exeter Academy Library, Isometric Plan, Exter, New Hampshire

FIGURE 4–13. The Carrels Inside
the Brick Donut

Photo: Howard D. Menashe

library had little to do with Kahn's spatial order. I found no user who spoke of the reading areas as places in which to take a book to sunlight. Eleven of the students felt that the perimeter carrels had some sort of secluded character to them, yet they did not see these carrels as "discovered places in the folds of construction." More than half of my eighteen interviewees were aware that the reading rooms and the carrels were separate in some way from the book stack areas. Yet only one student noticed that this separation involved a difference in brick versus concrete construction. Very few understood the book-carrel separation as the interface between two nested donuts.

I read Kahn's spatial order statement to them and asked them to respond to it. A few latched onto Kahn's terminology as a convenient, post hoc explanation for their understanding of the library.

The thing about the donut is good, but I wouldn't have thought of it.

About the three donut rings or something like that . . . I don't really understand that.

Then there was the student who picked up the term *donut* only to misapply it in his own understanding of the library.

From the outside the library is like a regular donut. And in here it is almost like a sugar donut. Outside it's plain and simple. And when you come in here, it's quite intricate.

In time I realized that there was a very simple reason why Exeter's users did not appear to experience Kahn's spatial order. These users did not generally understand library books in the same manner as Kahn had. For these users, library books were, by and large, not a part of an inspiration ritual. These students belonged to a top academic preparatory school where books were assignments. Books were to be read quickly, digested and analyzed, and dis-

FIGURE 4–14. Louis I. Kahn:
Central Space, Exeter Library

Photo: Howard D. Menashe

sected. For the Exeter student, books were "on reserve," "in the catalogue," or "due back in two hours." The carrels were places for hard work and studying. They were not usually places for solitary inspiration by reading. I asked the users if they felt invited when they saw the presence of books all around the central court; only a few said yes. Many were indifferent. Others found that presence distinctly distasteful.

The first time I came in the building I noticed the architecture more than anything else . . . I wouldn't notice the books first. I notice the books when I have to notice them, when I have an assignment to do!

FIGURE 4–15. Louis I. Kahn: Brick Exterior, Exeter Library

Photo: Jonathan Tsao

I think it is an invitation to see the books in the central court, but sometimes when you have a lot of work you have to do, a term paper you have to do, you don't want to go to those books.

Here people are going to be interested in books, whether they want to or not.

For Exeter's users, the library was not the chronic space for solitary inspiration with a book. Rather, it was a chronic space where students sought each other out for communal inspiration, much as in Kahn's spatial order for the school at Ahmedabad. Exeter had a student center nearby, a large building with institutional lounges for socializing. Yet the social center of the campus had moved to the library. In part, this was because students could avoid confinement to their rooms in the evening if they elected to go to the library. Yet the library's brick donut received and invited student socializing. Students began to rearrange the furniture of the brick donut, shifting chairs and sofas from configurations favoring solitary reading to configurations for intimate two- and three-person groups (Figure 4-16). The students mentioned how they came to the library for social interaction.

Students use this library a lot to come and meet friends. There's a lounge on the third floor which people use to study in, but there's always a lot of people and friends and stuff . . . It's not at all like a library.

A library has to have a reference section, and it has to have books. But I think it also has to be a place where you can get together and run bull sessions without disturbing the people who are attempting to work.

You can work together here, instead of by yourself. You can arrange to meet a friend from any part of the campus. It's a very useful place.

The library's central area, rather than having the invitation of books, had the invitation of meeting. Although a few students browsed the open books on the shelves overlooking the central area, more students stood there to look down into the court to see if they knew anyone coming into the library.

My friends and I have this special whistle. Whenever any of us enters the building, we whistle up from the court. And if we get a replying whistle from some place up above, we know we're here. We get together.

The central court had become a special place on campus. It became a place for rituals proclaiming the students' indifference to the serious work of books at their school.

FIGURE 4–16. Changes in Seating at the Exeter Library: (a) Original Isolated Public Seating, (b) Rearranged Intimate Group Seating

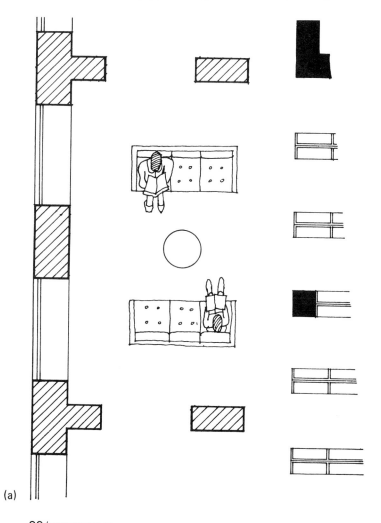

(a)

The other day, someone took a pillow off the third floor lounge and threw it all the way down to the main floor through the court—weird stuff here.

Last Halloween, a bunch of students did this amazing thing. They came and dumped a dead dummy they had made off the floors upstairs into this court. Then they left. Guerilla theater!

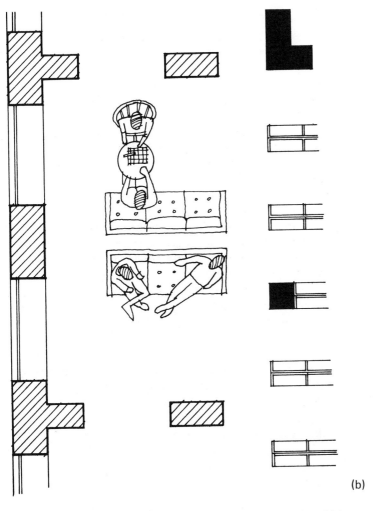

(b)

Sometimes someone will sit down at the piano down in the court and begin to play while everyone just goes their own way around him.

The central court became a place scheduled for concerts and ceremonies, events that used to be held elsewhere. It also became a place of sublime mystery, suggesting dimensions that existed just beyond the students' grasp.

There is something about the curvilinear entry stairs coming into the court. You want to go in. It's like a big mosque.

Every time you walk into the library, you still feel drawn to look up above you and gaze around. I really like it a lot. But it's so sacred!

Kahn intended the Exeter Library to be in chronic space for the inspiration of the individual with a book. Instead, Exeter was in chronic space for the inspiration of the individuals through meeting. In Kahn's spatial order, the central void proclaimed an invitation to a ritual with books. Books would be taken from the protective and dark inner concrete donut out to the peripheral brick donut and out to a sunlit, illuminated reading. For the student users, the central void proclaimed the meeting of friends. There, the users met and went out to the periphery for a bull session or communal studying.

As with House III, Exeter's users ignored Kahn's spatial order in their experience of the library. They installed their own spatial order of a library for inspiration through meeting. Yet Kahn understood his spatial order of the library as itself an instance of a more basic spatial order—inspiration. Kahn considered inspiration as a fundamental aspect of living and as the "beginning" of libraries. Inspiration was an interface or a threshold of two forces that resulted in illuminated materials and space.

Inspiration is where the desire to be/to express *meets the possible . . . I likened the emergence of light to a manifestation of two brothers . . . One is the embodiment of the desire* to be/to express *and one . . . is* to be/to be. *The latter is non-luminous and one . . . is luminous . . .*[19]

[19]Louis I. Kahn, "I Love Beginnings," *A+U: Architecture and Urbanism* (1975), p. 279.

The luminous turns . . . to flame, and flame deteriorates into material, and material becomes means, possibilities, the evidence. So therefore mountains are spent light, the streams are spent light, the air is spent light, you are spent light . . . The will to express and the will to make meet in a kind of threshold which . . . are the inspirations.[20]

To Kahn, a library was inspiration by books. So he saw individuals reading books comfortably, illuminated in sunlight at the exterior periphery of the building. To the users, library was inspiration by being with friends. They took their friends out to the naturally lit periphery to be with them in plush chairs. These users were responding to Kahn's more basic spatial order of "inspiration." The students that I talked to sensed that their library was more than just a student lounge and more than just a library. As one student said, the library was "more an institution than a collection of books." It had become a unique place to be on the Exeter campus.

The Exeter Library points out that when design proceeds on the basis of a profound spatial order, such as "inspiration," users are likely to find their daily experience altered and extended in some fashion. Despite the stigma of books at Exeter, the library still became a place for its users' inspiration.

In Chapter Three, we saw that we continually evolve our spatial order of the home in order to rethink our lives. In this chapter, we see that professional building, like lay building, uses spatial orders. The exotic and refined formal devices used by designers are simply means for manifesting those orders. As we have seen at the La Tourette monastery, at Broadacre City, and at Exeter, professional building by spatial orders becomes a way to rethink our social institutions. Professional and lay building inspired by spatial orders are attempts to rethink life spatially. At its worst, professional building interferes with its users' on-going chronic space experience. But at its best, professional building works with its users' space experience and deepens and enriches its users' lives.

[20]Romaldo Giurgola and Jaimini Mehta, *Louis I. Kahn* (Boulder, Col.: Westview Press, 1975), p. 15.

5
building
homes with
strategic
vision

In Chapter Four, we found that a fit between a designer's and users' spatial orders for the same building was not a prerequisite for a successful building. Now we will readdress this issue of the relationship between designer and user spatial orders and introduce the concept of strategic vision.

political interests in design

When user and designer interests clash in a design process, it is often common to argue that the designer should fit the design to the user. Fit theory assumes that the designer's job is that of a technician who identifies the user needs and translates them into newly-built environments.[1] Fit theory correctly points out that a professional designer must go beyond his or her interests to understand the user. Yet within the context of this book, we know that more is at stake in constructing environments than meeting so-called user needs. Constructing environments realizes deeply held, often subliminal spatial orders or expectations about how space should be configured. These spatial orders are based upon peoples' understanding of their lives and constitute nothing less than their life values in spatial form. So the relationship of spatial orders of participants in a design process is a relationship of social-spatial values.

Fit theory is inadequate in specifying the relationship between social-spatial values for several reasons. Fit theory assumes that what users want is on the whole self-consistent. But individuals' spatial orders need not be internally consistent or consistent with those of other co-users. Joan and her husband, in Chapter Two, or Jill and Henry, in Chapter Three, held quite different home spatial orders between themselves. It would be naïve for us to assume that spatial orders as social-spatial values are always in harmony and equilibrium. Consequently, there may be no definitive, overlapping set of user spatial orders by which to design.

Fit theory has other problems. In design, various spatial orders seek their own realization, and thus various psychological and social interests are at stake. In this

[1]Christopher Alexander, *Notes on the Synthesis of Form* (Cambridge, Mass.: Harvard University Press, 1964), Robert Sommer, *Personal Space* (Englewood Cliffs, N.J.: Prentice-Hall, Inc., 1969), and John Zeisel, *Sociology and Architectural Design* (New York: Russell Sage Foundation, 1975).

sense, the collection of spatial orders bearing on a design process represents a political engagement among differing values and interests. In design as a political engagement, it would be naïve for a designer merely to fit a project to its users oblivious of the interests at stake. Instead, a design process should be undertaken in which these interests are addressed with strategic vision.

A design process with strategic vision rethinks the client institution. The design process must sort through the range of spatial orders impinging on design. The spatial orders of some participants will seem trivial or illegitimate. Conflicting spatial orders must be clearly seen, some to be eliminated while others are retained. In design processes marked by strategic visions, designers and users re-envision their institutions for better or for worse.

But before there can be strategic vision in a design process, there must be strategic work. A good design process must possess designers willing to undertake strategic work to uncover the full range of spatial orders impinging on a design process. Because personal interests are at stake, designer and user groups maneuver to care for their own interests. Critical design information can seem to be presented in a straightforward manner in meetings or lectures. Yet, in time, it may become clear that information is being withheld, covered up, or altered to suit individual interests. This can happen as easily when a designer works with a couple living together as when a large design firm works for a huge bureaucracy. This nonforthcoming and frankly political aspect of design requires the designer and maybe the users to play detective, to do strategic work. Instead of design processes that blindly fit a design to its users, we must have design processes characterized by strategic work leading to strategic vision.

Now we will examine three small, residential design projects involving just a handful of participants, yet already confronting us with concealed and conflicted spatial orders.

the kitchen

In 1976, I received a commission to redesign a kitchen. It seemed to me a simple job. Bruce and Helen wanted more overhead cabinet space and were fed up with kitchen drawers that rubbed against each other, peppering food and utensils with sawdust. In our first meetings, Bruce took the position that aside from a few items, he was basically concerned with cost on the project. The kitchen itself was to be Helen's concern. Helen was a nutritionist and gave considerable thought to how her new kitchen should be arranged. I did my best to elicit useful information on the proper locations of shelves, drawers, appliance plugs, oven, and so forth. I was impressed with the care she gave to the kitchen details.

As I worked on the kitchen, I noticed that I was envisioning a very precise set of wood forms (Figure 5-1). I felt that I had introduced two formal devices into the kitchen. First, I decided to treat the kitchen as a cabinet-bounded space enclosed by, yet set off from, the existing mahogany, 1950s Bay region styled house. Second, to articulate that contrast, I made the kitchen cabinetry out of white birch with deep inset, dark horizontal bands that were the reverse of the birch bands applied to the mahogany living room cabinets.

It was only after all the drawings were completed that I came to understand how these formal devices realized the spatial orders of Helen, Bruce, and myself. I realized that I understood a kitchen to be a precise place, a place for the exact cutting of ingredients for Chinese food. I had created a kitchen with precise, crisply articulated cabinetry and work locations.

It took me months to realize that the sculptured, precisely banded kitchen realized Helen's unexpressed spatial order myth of a kitchen. It was not until she and I selected the kitchen sink that I understood the chronic space of her cooking rituals. She explained to me how the sink had to have unequal bowls with the small bowl to the left in order to keep the vegetables and meat sinks separate and noncontaminating. The kitchen I had designed had come to reflect her detailed kitchen zoning and pollution concerns. She was ecstatic about the materials and colors the kitchen took on. She said that the reciprocating horizontal banding was a "wonderful idea and, like good ideas, it was simple." She said the kitchen had a "tailored look" that she appreciated, because it fit with the rest of her house. She liked the fact that the living room remained mahogany while the kitchen became a white birch box. Helen was satisfied that the kitchen would indeed be a set-off place for the tailored, zoned, and efficient preparation of food.

I was continually surprised by Bruce. He was a successful, self-made businessman. Despite his professed lack of interest in the project, he became intensely concerned with different items. At first, the only way I could understand these interests was as a reflection of his past experience with buildings. He wanted special low heat, ballast fluores-

FIGURE 5–1. The Kitchen
Photo: Glenn Lym

cent lights and wanted to insure that all repaneled walls and new windows were fully insulated. Soon a pattern emerged in his off-and-on concerns for the project. Bruce was adamant in wanting to locate the breakfast area so that he could look out in the mornings over his view of San Francisco Bay, even if it made the resulting kitchen configuration awkward and more expensive. He was dead set against metal sliding glass doors. We settled for costly but more watertight sliding wood doors. I was further surprised when my suggestion to open up and skylight the kitchen ceiling was quickly appreciated by Bruce, although he had initially outlined a low budget for the project. I thought that opening up the ceiling would reinforce the spatial contrast of the birch box kitchen in a mahogany house and celebrate cooking by flooding the box with direct sunlight. It was several months before I realized that Bruce liked this design because it, like his other wishes, realized his spatial order of home as a protected skin for contents within. He was delighted with the possibility of improving the quality and insulation of that skin, while making it more penetrable with new vistas and entering light. Bruce's stated role as disinterested bystander merely obscured the fact that he, too, had a spatial order and wanted it included in the design. Through my collaboration with both Helen and Bruce, a kitchen design emerged that spoke to largely unconscious spatial orders.

But I had a problem. The contractor and I had determined that the cost for this kitchen would be 25 percent over the clients' last budget, which in turn was four times their initial budget. I got little sleep the night before we presented the price. However, Helen and Bruce decided to proceed with construction, stating that they understood the effect of inflation on costs and that the special items they had put into the kitchen justified the expense. They would not delete those items. I learned a good rule, that sometimes there is no such thing as a budget in a strict sense. It is a political item placed in circulation by a client to hold others in the design process in line. But when the design realizes a client's spatial order, the client will try to find the funds to pay for the project.

As this kitchen was being built, it occurred to me that the project had a dimension I had never seen before. The kitchen was a gift that Helen and Bruce were giving themselves, now that their children were grown and away from home. It was a gift to themselves as a couple. Although Bruce talked about how it might add to the resale value of the house, both loved it for what they wanted it to be. Their new breakfast area was well on their minds as the project neared completion. They were trying to decide on a new table and two chairs that would overlook their new view of the Bay. They had been used to eating with their children around a large dining table, and this would be their first two-person eating area. Without the three of us being aware, a design had emerged that entwined Helen's spatial order of a tailored and zoned kitchen with Bruce's spatial order of a more secure yet more open protective house shell, while creating a new chronic space—a daily eating place for just Helen and Bruce. They were renewing their relationship through me and the design process for their new kitchen.

STRATEGIC WORK. The design began as a straightforward attempt to obtain user needs by which to design a kitchen. Yet uncovering those needs led to deeper and never directly expressed spatial orders, which guided how the three of us made design decisions. Without my own or Helen's or Bruce's awareness, design was conducted at a spatial order level.

STRATEGIC VISION. In this project, the spatial orders did not conflict; they overlapped. The formal device of expressing the kitchen as a white birch box within a mahogany house shell enabled the design to realize simultaneously all our overlapping spatial myths. Our collective design vision emerged almost without our knowing it. It was a vision of the renewal of Helen's and Bruce's relationship.

the dark wood fortress

Two years later I began work on a remodeling to the thirty-year-old hillside house that David and Janet had built for themselves and their three children. Like Bruce and Helen, David and Janet now lived alone and wanted to rectify long-term defects in their housing. They wanted the severe earth settlement and related rainwater leaks of their house corrected. Their heating system no longer worked. David and Janet looked forward to their older days in a more comfortable, one level house.

Despite their emphasis on correcting functional defects, my clients also thought that it was time to enjoy the luxuries they had denied themselves for so long. David had worked hard all his life, first supporting his parents, then himself through school, and finally his own family. He wanted to rehabilitate and enrich his own castle. Janet wanted the house of her dreams, a collection of custom-tailored, individual spaces. They both wanted a more spacious living room, a new modern kitchen, guest rooms for their children's visits, a more gracious entry hall, a hot tub for themselves, and a bedroom befitting their clothes and magazine collections. They were articulate and gracious clients.

I began a series of meetings with David and Janet in which we talked out the spaces they wanted and began to sketch designs. At first I wanted to arrange the house with a flow of spaces from an uphill, existing outside terrace into a dining space into the living room and on out to a deck overlooking San Francisco Bay. But David and Janet did not like this arrangement. What was to me a marvelous and dramatic flow of space was to them a vulnerable house. As minorities of their generation, the exterior public world was not to be trusted. David had proudly built his own house after facing discrimination in their fruitless attempts to buy a house in the 1940s. David and Janet saw home as a protective oasis amid a prejudiced and exploitive world. My interest in an exterior and interior flow of spaces violated those spatial orders. Home to them implied an inscrutable wall presented to the outside, protecting a gracious interior. David and Janet did not want a house in active rapport with its surroundings.

As we proceeded, it was clear that their home spatial orders differed on important details. David saw his house as his court, responsive to his commands. When he hunted, he wanted a small room in which to prepare his ducks and store his rifles. When he cooked, he wanted a well-organized kitchen with the best equipment. When he turned on music, he wanted an imposing stereo system at his fingertips. Most of all, in his remodeled house, he wanted a commanding view from his favorite chair-place out over San Francisco Bay. He wanted to consume that view from his chair, to own it and thereby command it.

Janet's entry, powder room, living room, and dining room were on-limit places in which invited guests were made to feel at home, served wonderful desserts and meals, and surrounded by lovely artifacts. Her kitchen, bedrooms, and private baths were off-limits to all but the most immediate of family. There she stored her expensive collection of artifacts and clothing, often in a warehouselike disorder, quite out of keeping with the grace of her home's on-limit places. She was embarrassed by the off-limit spaces and felt exposed if guests ventured into them by mistake.

In her remodeled home, Janet wished to control her embarrassment and vulnerability. She wanted the house interior to be neutral and simple, quite a contrast to the gaiety of her home furnishings. She told me she could control and change her furnishings. But since she could not so readily control her home's surfaces once built, simple neutrality was what she wanted. Further, she sought semipublic spaces in her off-limit areas—a full entry space in the kitchen and a bay window sitting area in her bedroom to interface between her on- and off-limit places. She seemed to want her storage spaces constricted and moved into the corners and rear of the house. Her desire to control her vulnerability extended to her feelings about doors and windows. In keeping with her sense of house as an anonymous, protected domain, Janet requested all exterior doors open to public access to be solid, without windows. Yet, to survey possible guests, she wanted door peepholes. Janet's existing home had large floor-to-ceiling glass walls open to bay views. One might not have been aware of this upon entering that home, because those windows were totally covered by bamboo screens. She claimed that the sun's heat and possible neighborhood snoops made this necessary. If guests came to dinner, she sometimes would pull a screen, presenting a magnificent view to the diners.

It was clear that David and Janet differed in the details of how they saw their protected interior home. David saw a home with sites in which he could elegantly command and consume. He wanted a large living space in which he could sit comfortably and take in his view of San Francisco Bay (Figure 5-2a). In contrast, Janet was conflicted, wanting both to exclude as well as to include exterior views into her home. So she saw her public, on-limit spaces as a non-committal enclosure supporting her wonderful presentations to her family and guests (Figure 5-2b).

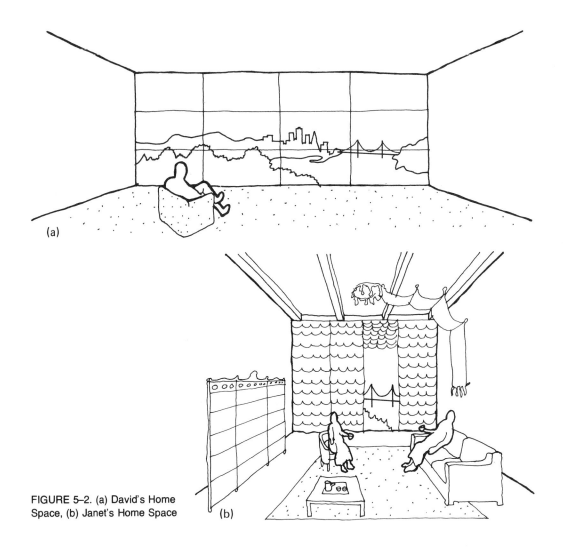

(a)

(b)

FIGURE 5–2. (a) David's Home Space, (b) Janet's Home Space

My design response began by honoring their long-formulated spatial order of an anonymous exterior protecting a rich interior. I felt that the relationship of interior and exterior had been and would probably remain problematic for them. Regardless of the fate of their windows, screened or not, I felt that their main interior spaces should be bathed in light to do justice to their wonderful presentations and to suggest some connection to the open outside sky. So I placed skylights over the support columns that would also vent summer heat (Figure 5-3). Janet protested; she could not easily screen these if she wanted to and the rain might make irritating noises. But I insisted and had good functional arguments for the skylights. I wanted to give the living room viewing windows a clear chance to be used. So I protected them, by exterior walls and screens, from summer sunlight and from neighbors' stares. Now there would be fewer excuses for David and Janet to close themselves to the outside.

David gave a name to their home spatial orders after he examined the drawings for the new foundations that would tie their home into solid soil. "It's going to be a fortress," he said. I hoped that the new house would root their lives more firmly in the ground at the same time as it opened their lives to the sky. Horizontally, I hoped it would become the dark wood command fortress with special devices by which Janet could more clearly deal with the interior's relationship to the outside world.

STRATEGIC ACTION. Through their discussions of the functional difficulties of their present house—settling, heat gain, inadequate storage—I was introduced to the background and intricacies of David's and Janet's home spatial orders. A design evolved that solved those concerns, as well as what was behind those concerns, namely the unfulfilled and distressed home spatial orders of David and Janet.

FIGURE 5–3. The Dark Wood Fortress Living Room

STRATEGIC VISION. David's and Janet's spatial orders were long-term creations that spoke to their experiences of racial discrimination, hard work and the creation of a wonderful interior life. It was time to manifest more fully these spatial orders and to clear up the material impediments to their home life. They wanted to reroot their home in a more solid earth. I wanted the color and verve of their interior presentations to guests to pervade their own private experience of home. I wanted to open their home to the sky, independent of their problematic relationship to the social world outside. I wanted to enrich and shed light upon their home.

All of us in the design process behaved with some degree of strategic vision. David was careful to allow his wife to express her feelings about screening windows, even though that threatened his desire for a commanding view. Janet spent days talking to friends, looking at houses, and examining magazines and drawings to uncover her real feelings about our designing. As the designer, I tried not to suppress the divergent energies of their home spatial orders, but to see and understand them clearly. I tried to design a home that would minimize the functional limitations of their old house, yet leave David and Janet free to work out their relationship to the outside. I tried to preserve the divergence and anxiety of their spatial orders. Yet, I also imposed a skylighted aura into their house that they could not understand from the vantage point of their own spatial orders.

In the same life-cycle stage as Bruce and Helen, David and Janet had overlapping spatial orders. In their remodelings, these couples sought to realize the details of home more fully. Differences between each spouse's spatial orders were largely accepted by the other spouse.

the small house   Concurrent with work on the kitchen for Bruce and Helen, I designed a small, inexpensive house on a very constricted (twenty-foot by ninety-foot) lot in Berkeley, California. I taped long interviews with each of my clients—Leslie and Paul—and observed their residential behavior patterns. They had jointly evolved a behavior pattern where their public life revolved around their living room. That was where they talked with friends, ate most of their meals, watched television, and played with their child. They talked separately about the spatial order of a barn. Leslie talked of a barn with wooden lifts above on which to sleep. It would be a styled, wooden home that separated public and private areas. Paul talked of a barn house having driftwood beams and swings on which he could move about and play. Rather than emphasizing Leslie's parceled-out spaces, Paul's spatial order of a barn emphasized movement, play, and transition.

I brought my own spatial order of a home to this design. In the several houses that I have designed and in the apartments my wife and I have rented, I have found myself seeing home as having central and peripheral areas. The center is communal space, a heart with eating and talking rituals. The periphery is private, personal spaces separated from each other, intense unto themselves, yet invisibly tied to something larger, the central area. I saw Leslie's and Paul's on-going living room activity as the center of their home.

Because the house could be no more than sixteen feet wide, rooms had to be arranged sequentially in a row. I created a central two-story living room space at the center of the site and placed other spaces on the periphery to the north and to the south. This created, from my point of view, two semiprivate towers on either side of the central public space (Figure 5-4). These towers were to be of wood with exposed joists and wood flooring in the celings, revealing the sleeping lofts above. I conceived of the central living room as an indoor-outdoor room lit from above, a snug living room in a large sunlit space in which Paul could climb and set up his gymnastic rings. I was very pleased that the design came quickly and spoke so easily to Leslie's and Paul's spatial orders of a barn and to my spatial order of a house with a center. But I sensed things were not quite right.

I went back to the interviews and carefully examined their comments on how they liked furniture arranged, how they used doors, and what places meant home to them. I discovered that there was more to the differences in their spatial orders of a barn than I had first realized. Leslie and Paul each had opposite ways of defining the places that constituted home. Leslie liked home places to have an explicit, well-defined focus, such as a well worked out furniture arrangement, nicely served hors d'oeuvres for visitors, or a closet for her child that could double as a play house. And she had explicit expectations about the boundary conditions of each home place. She wanted their bedroom and bathroom to be absolutely private. Those were places "for fantasy to occur." Yet she wanted a sense of contact with the living room when in the kitchen. Paul, on the other hand, did not care one way or the other for explicitly defined, focused, or bounded places. Whereas Leslie said she felt most herself in the bedroom or crafts room, Paul said he felt most himself wherever he happened to be, wherever his body wanted to go, and whatever it wanted to do. Leslie considered the living room and kitchen to be the core of their household. Paul considered that their household core involved the feelings people had and did not

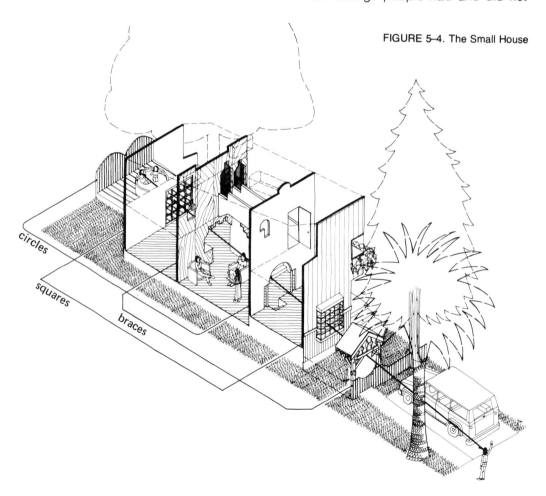

FIGURE 5–4. The Small House

circles

squares

braces

involve the physical structure of the home per se. Leslie stressed a home with explicit places; Paul delighted in place-to-place transitions. He had wanted to build a single-room, geodesic dome as a house. He thought that a one-room barn would be fine, for in such an area there could be minimal separation between places, perhaps just a low wall or a level change. When Paul became angry, he slammed doors and left home. When Leslie became angry, she went to a private room away from Paul. Paul had a spatial order of home as a set of found and evolving social situations. Flow, change, and escape were just as real to him as participation in any given situation. Leslie, on the other hand, had a spatial order of home as a set of explicitly structured situations. These spatial orders were at odds with one another and were the center of many conflicts between the two.

I fretted for a long time on the implications of this spatial order conflict. I felt that the house, in its design, should deal directly with this conflict and build upon it. At the time I was sketching large doorless openings from the two towers into the central living room. All of a sudden it occurred to me that in the formal device of a doorway lay the response to their conflict. It seemed to me that a doorway was a contradiction. On one hand, a doorway would be read as a part of a boundary, something closing off or making the edge of a place. Yet a doorway was also an invitation to flow into the next space. So, I introduced a set of doorway portals into the design from the entry gate in front through the house on out to the rear fence (Figure 5-5). On one hand, the feel of the small house was now extended outward in space. Paul could read the house as a flow of lightly delimited places. And Paul said to me, "It's a pleasure to wake up and move about in this house. I'll have to install a trapeze in the living room." On the other hand, the portals could also mark the boundaries of each room. Leslie remarked that "it is funny that I don't seem to mind that the crafts room does not have a solid door between it and the living room."

The final design had to reject the spatial orders of other design process participants. As a part of its decentralized neighborhood control policy, Berkeley required each new building project to receive a public hearing. Two neighbors became very upset at the prospect of a two-story home being built next to them. They had lived in San Francisco and thought of Berkeley as suburbia. The thought of a

two-story building where a one-story cabin had stood disturbed their reference community order of Berkeley as suburbia. This spatial order conflict was settled by the zoning board. Finally cleared for construction, the house then confronted the spatial orders of several contractors bidding for the job. These were contractors who were more craftsmen than mere builders and who had their own ideas about what a house should be. Several told us how they would alter the portals yet still "retain the charm of the original design." These contractors assumed the doorways to be pure decoration.

STRATEGIC WORK.   In this project, I hunted for spatial orders. Uncovering them took time. Leslie's and Paul's conflicting spatial orders were at first hidden and had to be sought out through careful post hoc analysis of early design discussions about the house.

In the kitchen, the fortress, and this small house, spatial orders influenced design, whether or not the design participants were aware of them. The first hint of an obscured spatial order was often through seemingly trivial and straightforward, functional comments by the clients, such as Leslie's remarks on solid doors or Paul's comments on stalking out when angry.

STRATEGIC VISION.   The spatial orders uncovered in Leslie's and Paul's home were treated in three ways. First, some spatial orders overlapped, such as the wooden barn fantasies and the centrality of the living room. These were condensed into the spatial order of home as an indoor/outdoor living room between two wooden towers. Second, some spatial orders conflicted, namely Leslie's sense of home as explicit places versus Paul's sense of home as transitional places. This conflict was preserved through the design device of the ambiguous portals. That device subdued conflict by realizing both spatial orders at once. Yet it also highlighted the conflict, preserving its energies for Leslie and Paul to deal with more clearly in the future. Third, other conflicting spatial orders were simply thrown out— those of the neighbors and the bidding contractors. In this small house, strategic vision addressed the clients' dreams while it grounded them in endemic marital conflicts.

conflicting spatial orders

The kitchen, the fortress, and the small house were small and simple design projects. Yet, as we have seen, the process of uncovering and of understanding spatial orders in these projects was complex and subtle. In the kitchen and the fortress, the design process dealt with overlapping and sometimes deliberately hidden spatial orders. In the small house, spatial orders overlapped and, moreover, conflicted.

The presence of conflicting spatial orders in a design process points out the inappropriateness of fit theory for design. When users bring conflicting spatial orders to design, there can be no simple fit of a design solution to the users' wishes. Strategic work is required to uncover and understand conflicting spatial orders. More importantly, conflicting spatial orders highlight the need for strategic vision in design. Participants in a design process must act with vision as they suppress or preserve conflicting spatial orders.

In the case of small residential projects, conflicting spatial orders offer material of legitimate importance to design. People who live together define themselves by contrasting as well as shared characteristics. Contrasting traits may form the basis of attraction among members of a living group.[2] With Leslie and Paul, complementary, personal characteristics were a basis of their long-term relationship. Leslie found Paul's sense of flowing and changing situations inspiring. She appreciated how he endured and celebrated situations that would have caused her great pain. Paul, in turn, relied on Leslie to maintain many of the situations of his life. Leslie reaffirmed her self-image of being a well-defined, articulated person by contrasting herself to the free-form character of her husband. And Paul reaffirmed the freedom he felt in his life by observing himself disengaged from the entanglements characterizing a part of his wife's life. In the design process for Leslie's and Paul's home, any attempt prematurely to edit and suppress conflicting spatial orders would have failed to see the social-spatial marital order that underlay their home life. In designing their house, I tried to address conflicted spatial orders directly and openly. I tried to recognize those conflicts as legitimate and fundamental parts to my clients'

[2]David Bakan, *The Duality of Human Existence* (Chicago: Rand McNally, 1966).

marriage. The design of their home attempted to embrace, clarify, yet not suppress conflict. My design tried to leave open the rich, yet conflicted ground of their marriage.

In the next chapter, we will consider more complex design processes involving large institutions. There we find even more instances of conflicting spatial orders impinging on design. Spatial order conflict is a critical issue in large-scale designing, which must be addressed by strategic vision.

6

**building large
institutions
with strategic
vision**

The focus of this chapter is the relationship between the spatial orders of designers, clients, and users during the design of large buildings. As we discussed in Chapter Five, the spatial orders or visions that guide how people shape space are spatialized social values. Thus, a design process is an engagement between different social values, a spatial political process. It is in this context that strategic action is necessary in a design process—the detectivelike work to uncover covert spatial orders impinging on a design. And it is also in this political context that design processes should have strategic vision—a wisdom in evaluating spatial orders for design purposes.

In the case of the design of large institutions, the complications of divergent spatial orders is far greater than in the case of single-family residential design. Instead of a single commissioning client, as in residential work, a large institution is composed of diverse user groups. Often the client group that meets with the designers is not the group that will ultimately use the completed structure. Institutions usually commission large design firms that are composed of diverse personnel, each with its own functions and outlooks. Needless to say, the possibilities for spatial order conflict are great in institutional designing. Strategic action becomes difficult. And the need for strategic vision becomes paramount to assimilate fully the fundamental institutional issues revealed in those spatial order conflicts.

In this chapter we will examine the design processes of three buildings, beginning with the case study of the design of interior office space in which spatial order conflict was ultimately ignored.

the ATT offices   Several years ago, I went to work for a very talented architect, Eugene Lew. I was a part of a team assigned to plan 180,000 square feet of new interior office space for a division of American Telephone and Telegraph in San Francisco. The clients for this project were a small group whom I will call the contacts. The contacts were formally responsible for liaison between the Lew office and ATT's departments and individual work groups. Beyond the contacts were the inner and the outer circles, groups composed of departmental representatives charged with decision-making responsibilities for design. Above them all was the division's head, an ATT vice president. The Lew firm was to design office space for 600 people, using information supplied by the contacts.

Lew approached this job with a well-developed understanding of strategic work. In dealing with institutional clients, Lew had found that information from the contact and user groups was not candid and, at its worst, deliberately deceptive. The contact and user groups manipulated information needed by the design firm in a way that controlled and manipulated the design to their own interests. To Lew, designing happened despite these struggles. Rather than seeing design as emerging from struggles, he saw design as the imposition of powerful design concepts upon these situations. Lew felt that design demanded that the architect possess political sense, strategy, and salesmanship in order to take control of the design process politically, and successfully impose the design.

For the ATT job, Lew devised a multiphased strategic work plan. In the beginning, he held a few meetings with the vice president, throwing out design ideas to pave the way for later decision making. But generally Lew stayed away from the job and sent out the team to sense the lay of the land among the contacts, departments, and work groups. We digested pages of departmental and furniture survey data, visited their existing offices, and engaged in months of negotiations to develop abstract adjacency plans, specifying the size, locations, and adjacency of all work groups on each floor. The contacts submitted to us their own versions of the adjacency plans for each of the 30,000-square-foot floors. These plans were worked out by them with the inner circle and specific work groups involved.

For the fifth floor, the contacts' adjacency plan showed the Operations Department's administrative wing with its computer group and computer in the northeast corner of the floor, far removed from the Accounting Department (Figure 6-1). Our data indicated that the Accounting Department also used that computer frequently. Further discussions indicated that the computer group at present was physically separate from its administrative wing parent. The assistant head of the administrative wing was about to lose his private office. The contacts insisted that a person of his rank should not have had a separate office in the first place.

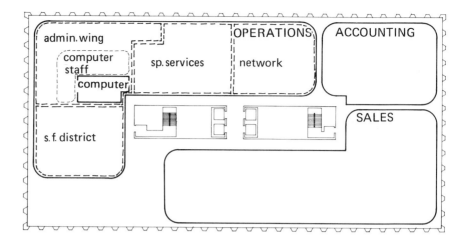

FIGURE 6–1. Eugene Lew and
Associates (EL+A): A.T.T. Space
Planning, San Francisco

This assistant head was intent on installing himself and his group along the north wall of the building with its fine view of the San Francisco skyline and in a corner location for maximum proximity to windows and for the prestige that such a location carried. He insisted that the computer group and computer take their places within the administrative wing, adding size and status to it.

On the basis of our functional data, we developed an adjacency plan in which we took the administrative wing out of the corner and placed it and the computer group next to the Accounting Department (Figure 6-2). In the process, the network group of the Operations Department was placed along the west wall of the building where it was within easy reach of the rear stairs that its personnel would use to get to work groups on the floor below. The San Francisco district group was given the northwest corner as it had no special circulation requirements and could be far removed from other groups, the elevators, and the stairs.

The fire code required each floor to have full height firewalls separating the floor into three 10,000-square-foot compartments connected only by fire doors. The architects and mechanical engineers for the building shell had indicated basic locations for these walls. In our adjacency plan, a firewall fell between the network group and the rest of the department. We sent our plan off to the contacts.

There ensued a protracted, in-house ATT battle. The administrative wing insisted on a corner location. The computer group thought it would be good to be near the Accounting Department and did not care about its connection with the administrative wing. Accounting seemed entrenched in its northeast corner, the prized corner of the building just below the vice president's suite on the floor above. The network group was considered by the administrative wing to be a definite part of its family, whereas the San Francisco district group was a recent addition to the department, with a head who by-passed the administrative wing and reported directly to a boss upstairs. So the contacts requested that the locations of the San Francisco district and network groups be switched so that the firewall would separate the San Francisco group from the rest of the department. We were told by the contacts to stop work on floor five. There was a major reorganization in the works at the highest departmental levels, and the proprietorship of all of floor five was in question.

A month later, the contacts handed us their own new adjacency plan for floor five (Figure 6-3). The boss of the Operations Department had taken control of the fifth floor sales group, giving him control of most of floor five. It turned out that the head of the San Francisco group was this boss's righthand man. In the new plan, the San Francisco group now got the coveted northeast corner, displacing the Accounting Department to the west wall. The administrative wing got its northeast corner back with its computer intact and now accessible to the displaced Accounting Department. The contacts instructed us to accept their plan. They had a vested interest in seeing the project flow quickly. The head of the entire division had given them a fixed completion date to meet.

FIGURE 6–2. EL+A: Floor Plan—A.T.T. Space Planning, San Francisco

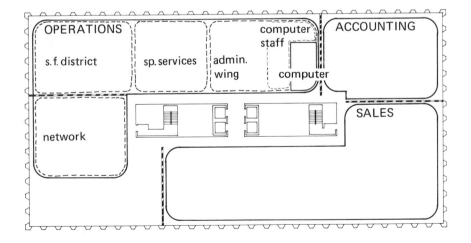

NORTH

Adjacency planning revealed the ATT user groups to be self-interested and territorial. They were not interested in their own user needs or office spaces with good views for all employees. It seemed to me that the operative spatial order at ATT was that of the territorial work group domain. Each work group sought a characteristic domain to control, proclaim their own values in, and by which to contrast themselves to other work groups. In the organization's existing office spaces as well as in our adjacency planning, the domains were articulated by firewalls, by the accumulation of desired status items such as corner locations or a computer, and by distinct decoration styles.

There were several characteristic domain decoration styles tied to differences in work group social structure and social values. Large work groups with high employee turnover rates usually had a clerical domain. There, individuals placed cute and personally meaningful objects on the walls, desks, ceilings, floors, and columns near their work stations. The net effect was a bombardment of apparent discordant images proclaiming individual work places. To the Lew office, clerical domains were evidence of the need for good visual order in the new offices.

Many of the technical work groups were in an austere engineers domain. There, desks were all in precise, daily maintained rows facing in one direction. Few, yet largely identical, objects adorned desk tops, and people sat erect in their chairs, the men in shirt and tie. The contacts had such a domain and continually wanted to impose their style

FIGURE 6–3. EL+A: A.T.T. Space Planning

NORTH

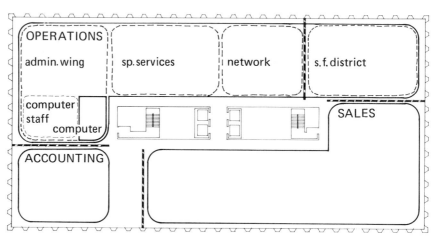

upon other work groups. They talked disparagingly of groups that took up extra space by having unusual desk arrangements.

Other technical groups had decorated engineer domains. In these groups, one or more individuals took it upon themselves to care for the group socially and decoratively. These individuals placed and maintained plants and posters and thereby decorated important circulation paths, entries, and vistas. This decoration was group-oriented and not individually oriented as in the clerical domains. One decorated engineer domain was maintained by a manager, who displayed a continually changing set of oil paintings done by friends and employees. In another group, a female engineer put up plants and posters throughout the domain and maintained a quip board that exhorted her male co-workers about sexism. These groups considered themselves distinguished by their decorations from the dull austere engineer groups. One variation on the decorated engineers domain was that of the ATT commercial art, filmmaking, television, and public relations groups. In these designer domains, individual decorations were sophisticated and hip and included items such as furniture and special entry doors never included in the decorations of the decorated engineer domains. Our austere engineer contact group had a running feud with the designer domains. The contacts were upset at the visual loudness of their spaces and suspicious of how those groups had acquired their elegant glass doors and furniture.

ATT's conference, reception, and lounge spaces were executive front domains, decorated by professional designers in the fashions of the time. These were showplaces to impress customers, consultants, and ATT employees. Behind these domains lay the individual offices, the executive domains, which were largely expressions of individuality not unlike that found in the clerical domains. Some offices were reminiscent of austere engineers domains; others derived from the designer domains, complete with prized sword collections or political pictures.

The work group seemed to me to be the basic building block at ATT. Its social composition and particular position within the ATT power structure determined its spatial order domain, its desires for a floor location, status objects, and

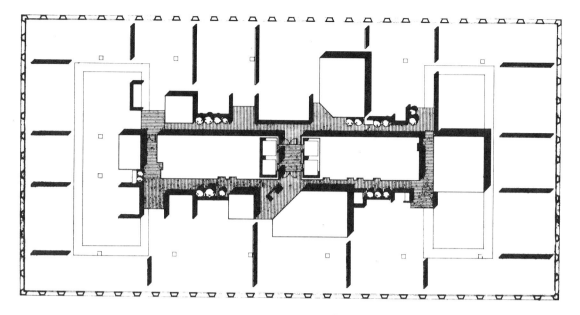

FIGURE 6–4. EL+A: A.T.T. Interior
Street Concept

decoration style. I felt that we should work with the spatial
order of work group domains, as they would be the basis for
how these groups reacted to our designs and for how the
group would modify the floors once they moved in. I hoped
that somehow we could design each floor as a quilt of
domains by recognizing and using each group's distinctive
domain spatial order.

But Lew did not agree. He reentered the scene and stated,
"Now we know more about how ATT works than ATT and
their contacts do. We are ready to design." Lew was interested in how to give each floor an overall, permanent
order. Whereas I was arguing to derive each floor from its
ecology of domains, Lew wanted to impose an overall pattern upon what seemed to him as time-consuming local
concerns. Lew and his associate quickly came upon the
formal device of locating permanently enclosed conference, office, and storage rooms around the elevator cores,
creating a ring street around that core and open office
space out to the window walls (Figure 6-4). Functionally,
this allowed the office work groups to expand and contract.
This formal device grew from Lew's spatial order of the
corridor as street. He saw the corridor as a reference
community. The corridor was to be a quiet lane recalling
brick-paved, urban streets with potted plants off of which
lay small boutiques and offices. To Lew, the overall order of
the floor was an enduring public order, a street with nodal

entrances leading to general spaces beyond. The order of domains was inconsequential.

Lew had carefully prepared the ATT executives to receive his design. The executives and the contacts were pleased. Like Lew, they were concerned with overall order, space efficiency, and minimal remodeling costs. Lew had created a spatial order tailor-made to his austere engineer clients' expectations.

The design team was now charged with working out Lew's design in detail, desk by desk, for each work group on each floor. In the ensuing months, much of the order of Lew's plan was eroded away. The work groups used the firewalls to assert and delineate their domains (Figure 6-5). Work group and department managers counted their firewalled domains and demanded to know why they received less space per employee than did their neighbors. Lew's design called for low partitions, interesting desk groupings, and large planting clusters to "break up" the otherwise large open desk areas. Slowly these items were lost. The contacts, true to their austere engineers style, gave the excuse that there were not enough funds to have these items. So work groups used to decorating their domains were thrown into large partitionless spaces with row upon row of like facing desks. In the end, the spatial order of the contacts, namely austere engineers domains, prevailed.

FIGURE 6–5. EL+A: Final A.T.T. Plan

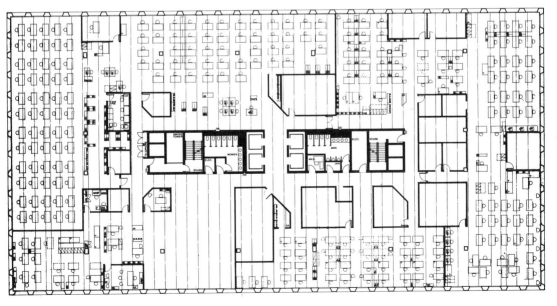

STRATEGIC WORK. Lew and his office exercised great skill in listening to and observing a large complex client-user. Despite this strategic work, the final design fell short of its goal, in part because the contacts ignored spatial orders divergent from their own. Skill in strategic work is not itself enough to ensure successful designing.

STRATEGIC VISION. At ATT, there was a conflict between the spatial order of an overall public order and the spatial order of work group domains. Rather than seeing this conflict as a legitimate part of ATT, the contacts and the Lew firm decided to squash that conflict. Lew's spatial order of the corridor-street ignored the spatial order of the work domain. And when individual work groups sought to impose their domain spatial order through any means possible during the later phases of design negotiations, the contacts made sure that those means would be minimal, drastically more minimal than Lew himself had wanted. By attempting to squash conflict, the contacts had ensured its future continuation. In later skirmishes, departments and work groups would vie for domain space and partitions.

A more successful design might have been based on spatial order conflict. A formal device might have been found that would have created an order of the street out of an order of conflicts between groups and departments competing for space along the street. Then wall, partition, and status objects competing along the corridor-street edge would have orchestrated and enlivened the corridor-street, rather than being masked and destroyed by that street. By directly addressing the conflict, an endemic territorial issue at ATT would have been clarified and exploited for the benefit of all. The design process at ATT, while having superb strategic work, lacked strategic vision.

Kresge College

Kresge College was in planning from 1966 to the early 1970s at the University of California at Santa Cruz. The UCSC campus was located in a redwood forest overlooking the Pacific Ocean. It had been modeled after Oxford and Cambridge universities in which a university is made up of numerous small colleges that house and offer core instruction to its students. Kresge was the fifth college to go into construction at UCSC.

When architects Charles Moore and William Turnbull began to work on Kresge's design, no faculty had been hired to staff Kresge nor were any students enrolled. The architects' client was the UCSC administration and its in-house project-architects staff. From the beginning, Moore and Turnbull wanted a less institutional and more personal living and educational complex than the more formal, early UCSC colleges. So they proposed breaking up Kresge's public and academic functions and dispersing them among the living units.

As in their New Haven low income housing complex done at the same time (and discussed in Chapter Three), Moore and Turnbull developed an urban street spatial order for Kresge. It came to them at their first site visit, which for Turnbull was an experience in acute space. At the site, Moore and Turnbull walked in opposite directions in the wooded ravine. When each returned to the ravine, they exclaimed, "This has to be a street!" For Turnbull, this was an inspired moment, a civilized sharing between two people in the middle of a forest. Thus came their spatial order of Kresge as an urban community in the forest, as an Italian town in the wilds, and as a place for protected civil street encounters in the redwoods. The college was not to be institutional nor was it to be rural and provincial. Instead, a lively and inspired urban scene was to weave itself throughout the complex, thereby allowing a more even distribution of public and private places and academic and residential places. Moore wrote

The scheme . . . was based on a pedestrian street winding up the ridge in the forest tightly flanked by buildings, their fronts painted white to bring light into this passage in the dark forest . . . The imagery of whitewalled galleries along a winding street is, of course, of a village.[1]

Their earliest scheme for Kresge was a bridgelike structure that spanned the ravine with rooms along the outer edges and a pedestrian street in the middle. Another scheme consisted of two three-story buildings flanking both sides of

[1]Kent C. Bloomer and Charles W. Moore, *Body, Memory and Architecture* (New Haven, Conn.: Yale University Press, 1977), pp. 115–116.

a pedestrian street, a serpentine form making its way through the UCSC forest with parking below (Figure 6-6). Library, food service, administration, lounge functions, and classrooms were on the street as were the various lounges and living rooms that led to sleeping accommodations above. Moore and Turnbull took their designs to a third major scheme and developed a full set of construction

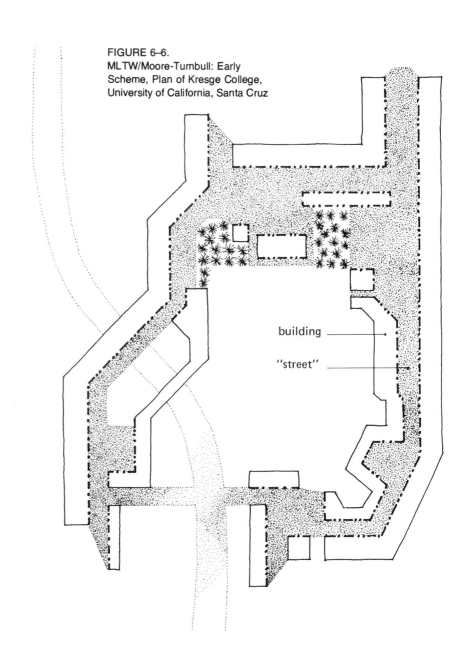

FIGURE 6–6.
MLTW/Moore-Turnbull: Early Scheme, Plan of Kresge College, University of California, Santa Cruz

building

"street"

drawings based on it. But by then California had elected a new governor, who cut funds for the University. Kresge's construction was shelved temporarily.

In the meantime, UCSC hired biologist Robert Edgar to become Kresge's provost. Edgar came to UCSC with great expectations to build a residential and academic community that would combine the humanistic social sciences and the physical sciences with an environmental studies program. The college and its growth was to be the central concern of that studies program. Edgar believed that Kresge should evolve from its interpersonal roots rather than begin with an imposed and built academic and administrative order.

We were purposefully trying to develop organically. We wouldn't know its overall shape until we had developed that large and seen what that large was like . . . To me that meant developing in as open a way as possible, where individuals that are working within the college at any one time see themselves as having the capacity of changing the structures that are operating.

With forty students and three other faculty members, Edgar spent a year developing a curriculum plan, interviewing faculty, and working with Moore and Turnbull. Edgar and his class developed the "kin group," which was to be the interface between the individual and the college. The kin group was to be ten to fifteen males and females living together as freshmen and assigned to the same faculty advisor. Later, they might live separately or even off-campus, yet still be tied by their freshman experiences just as in an extended family or kin group.

Edgar had developed his own spatial order for Kresge. He wanted separate buildings for each kin group, each with bedrooms and a central eating and communal space. Furniture was to be maximally flexible, enabling students to set up their personal areas and kin communal areas as they wished. Flexibility was to characterize the overall college layout as well. If community was to emerge organically from its pieces or kin groups, the buildings of that community had to be flexible. Edgar envisioned a set of buildings that could be dismantled and moved every so often. He saw barn-raisings throughout the life of Kresge, celebrating its piecemeal growth. He wanted what he called a "tinker toy college" that people could rebuild every so often and that in time would find its own spatial order.

Edgar's spatial order of the tinker toy college ran into three obstacles. First, the UCSC administration balked at the idea of rebuildable buildings. The University was not interested in what it saw as another flexible, modular building fiasco. Second, Edgar found that the administration's project architects interfered with his direct communication with the architects. He understood strategic action and bypassed the project architects to deal directly with Moore and Turnbull. Third, Edgar's spatial order of the tinker toy college had to contend with the architects' spatial order of the urban street village in the forest.

The provost and the architects' spatial orders complemented yet conflicted with each other. Edgar was pleased yet dismayed with Moore's and Turnbull's early designs. The architects' dispersal of residential, academic, and communal functions within a village in the forest pleased Edgar's sense of a growing, organic college. But the architects' organizing urban street left him cold. He did not want the college's overall order predetermined. To him, the street was just one of many ways to arrange the buildings on the site. The street offended him with its massive multistory, long serpentine buildings moving through the forest.

In the meantime, the architects had found that the residential, classroom, and special activity spaces were each to be funded by different federal, state, and private funds. These separate functions had to be in individual structures, so that if funds for one dried up, the others' construction would not be jeopardized. This, along with a newly constricted budget, led the architects to abandon the long mega-buildings of their early schemes and go to smaller, separated two-story buildings, requiring less site preparation during construction (Figure 6-7). Moore and Turnbull resorted to large free-standing, projecting walls to create their continuous urban street (Figure 6-8). For Turnbull, fragmentation of the buildings was an unfortunate event that had to be lived with. For him, it was the overall social-spatial order of the street that was important. That had to be saved in the new design.

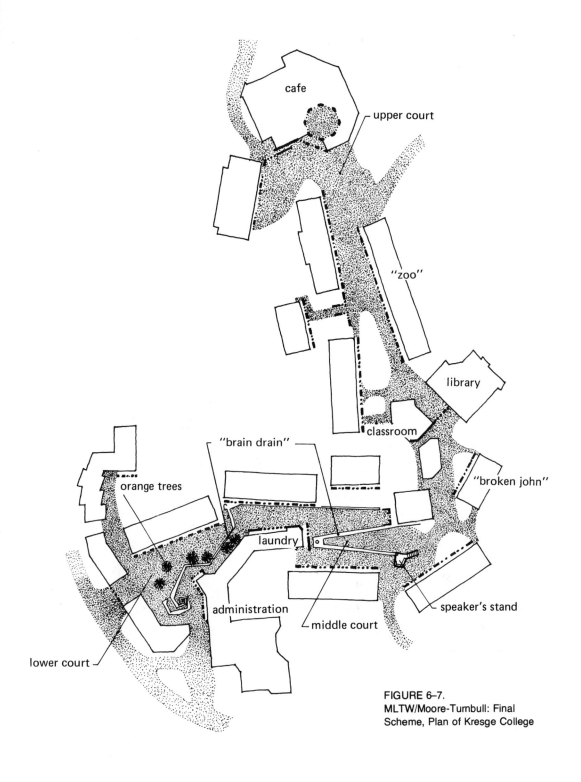

cafe

upper court

"zoo"

library

classroom

"brain drain"

"broken john"

orange trees

laundry

speaker's stand

administration

middle court

lower court

FIGURE 6–7.
MLTW/Moore-Turnbull: Final
Scheme, Plan of Kresge College

We were responding to the pragmatism of how the hell we could get the buildings in and afford to build them and maintain our street which we fought for the whole time. The street was the important idea we were not going to compromise on. So Kresge got to be more picturesque than it was earlier as it got to be more practical. For us, the issue was how do you make community? A community is oneness. You've got 650 diverse individuals in a community. How do you make a physical place whose overwhelming statement is "you are a community," that is, "you are a street"?

However, the fragmentation of the buildings pleased Edgar, for it realized his spatial order of little buildings set in the forest. Edgar remained indifferent to the street itself.

I felt good about the way the form of the college fragmented. I really liked that. And I think it worked to the advantage of the people in the college. Turnbull had talked about the street as an urban place. But I didn't think about it. I didn't have feelings one way or the other about that.

FIGURE 6–8.
MLTW/Moore-Turnbull: Kresge College

Photo: Glenn Lym

Unlike ATT, Kresge's architects and users managed to circumvent the intervening client—the UCSC administration and staffs. The architects and the users had conflicting spatial orders, yet, through direct contact, an ambiguous forum—the street with its fragmented buildings—arose, responding to those conflicting spatial orders. The architects saw the street as the overall order of the community and the fragmented buildings as a practical necessity. The provost saw the street as a practical necessity and saw the fragmented buildings as the embodiment of a community whose order derived from its social units. The architects and the users were somewhat aware of their fortuitous responses to each other. Turnbull recalled

I don't remember any negative reaction that the Kresge people had to the street. It was sort of the same way Chuck Moore and I sort of looked at each other and said, "Yeah, that's it." It was always "that's a super way to organize it." It felt right to everyone so there was never any negative play.

Edgar commented

I thought Turnbull had a very strange image of what he wanted to do and it was sort of his idea. So he talked in terms of the abstract values that we saw as important in the college, but translated those into his own images. I always felt he was a really neat guy who understood what we were trying to do. But on the other hand, he was doing things his way. I felt that there wasn't a matching somehow, yet there was a kind of empathy there at some kind of level.

In the winter of 1976, I interviewed twelve students, males and females, living in all locations at Kresge. These were second-generation Kresge students, in love with, yet irritated by Kresge. As second-generation students, they did not share the interests of Edgar and his early students.

These second-generation students led a life that might be called "California mellow." They came to Kresge to enjoy what was to be found. They were passive, expecting to get from and not to give to the Kresge community. They were not the self-motivated individuals that Edgar had envisioned coming to experiment with and discover self and community. Only one of the twelve students talked of coming because he wanted to participate in the creation and growth of an educational community. All the others said they had come because, compared to the other UCSC colleges, Kresge had a looser and more communal social life, because Kresge and UCSC were less high pressured academically than other university campuses, and because Kresge provided them with their own kitchens so they did not have to hassle cafeteria eating. As a group, these students were unconcerned about developing an inquiring community order for Kresge. They were self-oriented and focused on the particulars of their social life.

The students liked the way residential, academic, social, and administrative functions were distributed throughout the college. Like the architects, they felt it reinforced their sense of living in a sociable place.

Kresge has been compared by people to the old Italian towns, which I think is a useful comparison.

It is strange trying to figure out why they built the things they built in this place. But it is less centralized than the other colleges. It makes you feel the whole place is more integrated as a whole.

They valued the order of the kin group living units that gave them a sense of living in a personalized environment. Ironically, like Edgar, they liked the fragmentation of the buildings, because it reinforced the personal and small group qualities they liked in the college.

This place building-wise is more personal than the other colleges at UCSC. In the other colleges you're just another one of four giant walls around a square court. Here each building is separated.

Kresge is better than the other colleges partly because of the architecture. It's not so blocked, not so much one big block of a building next to another block as the other colleges are.

Yet these students liked Moore's and Turnbull's street, not because of its civic qualities, but because it provided them with a way to have fun with themselves, as this freshman pointed out.

I like the street. My friends and I skateboard a lot down it. Have you ever heard of frisbee golf? You throw a frisbee through the holes in those big walls like those square holes over the street. It's usually a par three from the coffee house at the top of the street to the library holes.

The street provided them with wonderful, personalized social situations for seeing people on balconies, being seen from your own balcony, spying on friends, and informal, spontaneous hanging out (Figure 6-8).

Ironically, the provost and the architects had more in common with each other than with these second-generation students. Like Edgar, Moore and Turnbull had expected that Kresge would generate a public order in which self would be inspected socially. In their spatial order of the urban street, the architects expected a truly public and nonpersonalized street activity. The private room was to be a place for the individual, while the street was to be a place for the public.

At Kresge, the boundary between a student's introspective self and public self was problematic and in temporary suspension. None of the students that I talked to had come to Kresge to develop the scrutinized self or community envisioned by Edgar. The students enjoyed the street for the informal, personalized social situations it created. But they rejected the street as a public order. To them, what occurred on the street was not all that different from what occurred in their living units. They disagreed with Turnbull's intent that large balcony openings had been designed to present the individual to a public out in the street (Figure 6-8). Turnbull remarked

You have got to think of the super openings on the units sort of as great frame windows of appearances. They take you as a single individual above and make you special much the same way as in an old street.

To the students, there was no individual or public to present to each other. In response to Turnbull's remarks, they commented

I don't see what he says happening. I don't see that the openings put people on a pedestal.

I could see that, but I would see more a group of people, like three or four people framed. So I see those frames as open, not making the individual special. I see those openings and the architecture here as providing a sense of community—everything larger and more open.

Not concerned with either the scrutinized self or the overall public order of their college, these students had their own spatial order for Kresge. For them, Kresge realized the spatial order of a forested retreat. They considered Kresge to be embedded in the whole UCSC campus and its forest, which in turn was separated and protected from the problems and realities of the metropolis and nation outside. Kresge was a place for suspending concerns about the realities of the outside world as well as a place for suspending commitment to self and to community. Thus, the students objected to Turnbull's discussion of the orange trees that populated the street's lower court (Figure 6-9). To Turnbull, the street was an urban and public place set in the midst of, yet protected from, the forest.

What the orange tree does in a redwood forest is to really say, hey, I'm a hothouse thing. I'm really inside, protected and loved and cared for, the same way that anybody in that street as a part of a community of social beings is protected in the nineteenth-century sense from the wild outside terrorism landscape.

FIGURE 6–9.
MLTW/Moore-Turnbull: Kresge College

Photo: Glenn Lym

But to those second-generation students, Turnbull's remarks violated their spatial order of the comfortable, forest retreat.

I do think of it more as Kresge being protected from the outside world. I really don't think it's that protected from the wild landscape.

Well, I think his analogy or metaphor there is kind of silly, I mean about the orange trees. But it does give you a sense that this is a fantasyland or something different from the rest of the world. We call this place candyland. I don't think the inside street versus the forest is a meaningful separation.

The trees are protected like having a pet. Some pets are luckier than others. They get into a space where they are fed and loved. They have a good life. I think Kresge has that element of protection, which I personally rebel against. All of UCSC is very up-on-a-hill, very elitist, a monastery atmosphere, and Kresge in particular. I don't particularly like the idea of being removed from the actual goings on of the outside world.

The students objected to the street's whiteness, because it worked against their spatial order of the forested retreat. They liked the sociability of the street, but wanted it merged into the forest. They wanted to erase all traces of the street's public, civic nature.

Kresge really doesn't blend into the redwood too well, because it is painted white. The back sides are painted brown, which is better. The place really doesn't fit into the forest well.

I don't relate to the street as a protected place in my everyday living. That's not my awareness. The street is just too white. Streets happened along 2,000 years ago. Forests have been going on a lot longer. The street would have been more congruent with its environment had it been a natural finish like wood. The paint provides a feeling of this being a little city right in here.

I would have preferred anything but this white on the street. Maybe it's not because it reflects so much, though it is very bright. But it gives you a feeling of civilization. But I think you still know you're in the midst of these beautiful redwoods.

STRATEGIC WORK.   Much of the strategic work at Kresge was done by Provost Edgar. He made sure that he had direct access to the architects, circumventing the UCSC administration. Then he created a class of students and faculty to plan Kresge in conjunction with the architects. The direct lines of dialogue were largely responsible for how skillfully Kresge's design addressed its architects and first users' overlapping and conflicting spatial orders.

STRATEGIC VISION.   The strategic vision in Kresge's design process was its grasp of its essential spatial order conflicts. The architects saw an enlightened public order in the trees, a college quite unlike its institutional forerunners. Edgar and the first-generation students saw a tinker toy college where self, kin group, and community were to grow and be examined. The architects posed the issue of how to come to terms with the overall organization of the college. They worked hard to give Kresge its public street. Edgar posed the issue of attention to self and to details that would grow an overall order in time. Edgar and his students introduced a useable private and kin group order into Kresge. Both spatial orders were two facets of a vision of education based on attention to the intimate and the public order of meeting in a forest.

Through the direct dialogue established between the architects and the users and through the architects' continual skill in making the best of years of changes and budgetary constraints, a design emerged that embraced the vision of its creators. Conflicting spatial orders were not eliminated as at ATT, but embraced. An ambiguous formal device—fragmented buildings connected by free-standing street walls—realized conflicting spatial orders.

Kresge's second-generation users were intent on realizing their own spatial order of a forested retreat in which to suspend an examination of self and community. The challenge of Kresge's built-in conflict between overall order versus organic order went right past them. In Kresge, the original designers and users created a built-environment of deeper vision than displayed by its second-generation users.

Provost Edgar realized that Kresge's later students were not committed to his vision of the college. In time, he resigned his post. To him the difficulty was not with students, but with faculty concerned with their own disciplines and tenure possibilities. Ironically, despite his objections to the street as an imposed order, it was the communal order of the street and its urban color that was Edgar's solace upon leaving Kresge.

[Faculty] people said anything to get here. Most academic people want a traditional environment. And once they were here, they did anything they wanted to unless you had sanctions over them. In a lot of ways, I wasn't successful. Academically, the college was a failure. I think I was successful in helping create a living community that had certain kinds of attributes to it that are still staying on to some extent. You know, maybe just the bright colors are enough to give the students that sense of specialness now.

In forging and building upon conflicted spatial orders, Edgar, Moore, and Turnbull created an environment whose vision went beyond that of any of their spatial orders alone and beyond that of Kresge's subsequent users.

The architects of ATT and Kresge both put forth spatial orders of the street. The street is an excellent vehicle for ordering the relationship of individual groups to a public whole. Lew stressed the overall clarity and uniformity of streets. His street of offices tended to suppress the territorial order of work domains. Moore and Turnbull also stressed the overall order that a street gave Kresge. Yet their street accepted the parochial interests of small scale, user groups. The street created by the provost and his architects could be understood as both a clear, overall organization of the Kresge community as well as an individualistic ordering of its parts.

Marin County Civic Center

At the Marin County Civic Center, Frank Lloyd Wright and his clients employed a spatial order of the street to bring a new overall political order to a county government. Unlike the ATT and Kresge case studies, Wright and his Marin clients, from the beginning, communicated directly with each other by means of spatial orders.

The suburban county of Marin across the Golden Gate Bridge from San Francisco began work on a civic center in 1959. It was to be one of the last buildings designed by

Frank Lloyd Wright. The process of this center's design was a story of a conflict between two fundamentally different views of county government, each seeking to realize its own spatial order in the design of the civic center. This design process was an overtly political process marked by crucial elections, recalls, public rallies, and protest meetings. In response, Wright, then in his late eighties, spoke out, putting forth and publicizing spatial orders. His strategic work was not as clandestine as Lew's or as straight ahead as Provost Edgar's and Moore's and Turnbull's. At Marin, Wright simply pointed out how the spatial order of a civic center should be part of a larger spatial order for the whole county. Wright inspired the county to a new understanding of itself through their design of the civic center.

With the opening of the Golden Gate Bridge, World War II and the postwar economic boom, Marin was opened to an influx of people seeking housing and county services— hospitals, roads, sewers, schools, police protection, libraries, and so forth. Going into the 1950s, Marin's political factions responded to the postwar demands in distinctly different ways.[2] The localites wanted county power to remain in the hands of existing institutions. Localite politics were based on an informal relationship of males rooted in Marin business ventures. Growth for localites was not an evil per se, as long as it helped local institutions and increased county revenues. By the 1950s, a county supervisor, N. Fusselman, was a leader of this faction.

In contrast, the reformers argued that Marin's growth created major policy questions. The amount and location of industrial and residential development had to be controlled. A program to conserve Marin's forests, seashores, mountains, and streams had to be adopted. The county government had to be overhauled. The reformers advocated a central county administrator to replace the practice of having the five county supervisors run the county, administering their own districts, sometimes with patronage involved. The reformers wanted the county offices collected from thirteen locations and located at a single civic center site. Vera Schultz was a prime reform leader. In 1953, she was elected to the board of supervisors.

[2] Evelyn M. Radford, *The Bridge and the Building* (New York: Carlton Press, 1974).

That year, the reformers held four of the five supervisor seats. Over the objections of Fusselman, they voted to create a central county administrator. The board began a protracted fight over the location for a new civic center. Fusselman wanted the site in downtown San Rafael, the existing location of the county's offices. And he wanted the commission to go to local architects. The localites wanted the center to be a tall, imposing skyscraper, realizing their spatial order of a "back room" government, distant yet impressive to its populace. The reformers had a different spatial order for the center. They looked for large, nonurban sites outside downtown San Rafael. Mary Summers, Marin County's director of planning, suggested a grouping of low rise county buildings in a campuslike manor at such a site. The reformers sought a spatial order for the center that would be inviting to the populace and stimulating to the county workers assembled there. Summers remarked

We were thinking about a home, a central core, an inspiration for the county of Marin. It would be a family room, the place we all met together to do our business, to play, to have cultural activities.

After much fighting, a 140-acre site next to a large freeway outside San Rafael was purchased in 1956.

The board assigned Summers the task of chairing the committee to select an architect. She was looking for an architect who could realize the reformers' spatial order. She interviewed at least twenty-four architects from Marin and from all over the country, but was disappointed.

None inspired me or gave me any sense that this was the architectural firm or architect which we should have in Marin County. I would ask what would they be thinking about as they began to design our building, and they would say, "Well, it would depend on when your project came into the office who would be assigned to design it."

Mary Summers's husband suggested to his wife and to reform leader Schultz that they try Frank Lloyd Wright. Mr. Summers was a civil engineer born in Chicago, whose mother had attended Wright's lectures in the early 1900 Prairie House years. Excited, the reformers contacted architect Aaron Green, Wright's San Francisco representative.

On the recommendations of Schultz and Summers, the board of supervisors minus Fusselman voted to consider Wright alone for the job. In 1957, Wright met the supervisors for the first time in Green's San Francisco office. Fusselman was not present. Green recalled the meeting as a typical Wright-client presentation. But to the supervisors and Summers, the meeting was catalytic. Without having seen the site and with just the barest of details about the project's scope and requirements, Wright presented his ideas and his past work and convinced the supervisors that he was the architect meant to realize their spatial order of a reformist civic center. Summers recalled

That meeting was a fantastic experience. He simply inspired us all. He would work until we were satisfied. He wanted a perfect building, and he wanted us to have the perfect solution, which I thought was fantastic. He spoke about the building's fitting into their environment, suiting the kind of people who were going to be using it. This was the first time that an architect had begun to even speak in these terms to us.

Wright had sensed in the reformers an affinity to his own long-nurtured spatial order for the American city and its government. As discussed in Chapter Four, Wright's ideals were embodied in his spatial order for Broadacre City. There, the city would be decentralized and brought back to the land. Each family was to have its own dwelling rooted on its own cultivated acre. Markets, cultural events, business and civic administration buildings were to be scattered as jewels in a rural countryside. Wright saw the reformers' struggles with Marin County's exploding postwar growth, with Marin's threatened forests, meadows, and beaches, and with the localites' emphasis on old power structures as struggles of a people groping for a new spatial order—his spatial order of Broadacre City.

Three months later, Wright came back to sign his contract and take his spatial order to the Marin public. He spoke to a crowd of over 700 people and focused their attention on the gravity of their decision to hire him to build their civic center. He pointed out that what was at stake was the entire future of the county, which had implications for the nation and world as well. As he had done with the supervisors earlier, Wright inspired his audience by expanding their understanding of their immediate circumstances through spatial orders. Wright extolled his audience to examine his spatial order of Broadacres and a Broadacre-like civic center.

I feel I have come here on a mission to save Marin County . . . Citizens are going to give up their cars or they are going to give up the city. They will give up the city, because the city doesn't mean much to them now when they can get everything they had in the old-time cities and stay right at home . . . What you need is space, broad spacing on the ground . . . I see in Marin County this new space opportunity and before you, a great chance for free, open spacing . . . Your civic center should not have the usual ominous ring . . . like [a] center of business [or look] . . . as though everything was jammed [into it with] everybody . . . standing in everybody else's way.[3]

He capped off his talk by comparing Marin County to Bagdad, where he was designing a cultural center and university, and making reference to the localites' spatial order of the civic center as an imposing skyscraper.

At present I happen to be doing a cultural center for the place where civilization was invented, that is Iraq . . . Now, the city has struck oil, and they have immense sums of money . . . [But] they are not likely [to bring back their old culture] . . . because a lot of western architects are in there already building skyscrapers all over the place . . . So it seems to me vital over there to try and make them see how foolish it is to join that western procession. I think it would be foolish too for Marin County to join that procession. . . .

Wright's talk was well received by the crowd. His strategy to spur the citizens onto a better if not new vision of life in the county through their comprehension of what it meant to build a civic center paid off well, as future political events would tell.

The localites were ready for a protracted war against the reformers and their architect. In a last-ditch effort to abort the Wright contract, Fusselman supported a move to hire

[3]From Frank Lloyd Wright's Marin County public lecture, July 31, 1957, transcript by Mary Summers.

Los Angeles architect Richard Neutra. Later, Fusselman would conduct public interviews with a Wisconsin politician, who would warn Marin County of the budgetary evils of Wright buildings. The defunct Marin Taxpayers' Association would be reformed to block acceptance of the Wright plans.

The first major incident in this war came a day after Wright's public address. He was to speak to a formal meeting of the board of supervisors. In the front rows were members of the Marin American Legion Council, who stood up and announced that they had a dossier on Wright's World War II support of Communist activities. They insisted that no Communist should design Marin's civic center. At this, Wright proclaimed himself a loyal American and walked out of the chambers, perhaps out of principle and perhaps as an astute political move to galvanize his reformist support and squash the localite offensive. In any case, the project's future was momentarily at stake. Summers went after Wright to save the commission.

That afternoon, Wright paid his first visit to the site. He walked the land with his clients, the supervisors, and the heads of various county departments. For Summers that visit was an acute space experience. She was with a great man who was about to realize her dreams for a home for her county at the top of that hill.

Wright talked to each of the department heads on the site, asking them what they wanted the center to express. Summers recalls how she responded to his questions and how a chance incident with children indicated Wright's understanding of her remarks.

I said to Mr. Wright that it should be a friendly building, so that the public didn't feel repelled by it, because we were their servants. He grinned broadly and said, "Mary aren't you expressing yourself, the way you feel towards people you know?" A little later, I was right beside Mr. Wright and some children came up. They asked what was going on. And Mr. Wright lovingly reacted to the children. He said, "We are thinking about what you are going to have here as a civic center for Marin County. There are going to be things in here that you will love to do." Now the kids love their lagoon and the sort of rapids that he created and the ducks in the lagoon.

Like Moore and Turnbull at Kresge, Wright developed his spatial order for the civic center during his first site visit. Summers talked about that. She was pleased that the spatial order's receptivity to pedestrians and cars addressed her expectations for the center as a friendly place.

When we came down from the hill, he said, "I have the idea. You are going to be surprised at what I do with cars." Later, when I saw the plans, there would be cars driving through the building, able to stop inside the building and let out passengers, stop right inside the building! That was what he conceived the first day he was on the site.

Rather than understanding the site-derived spatial order as stemming from discussions with future users, architect Green felt that Wright was inspired by the site itself.

In about twenty minutes, Wright determined the synthesis of the design of the building and explained it to me. The basic inspiration came from the site—that this is the site of rolling hills. He said, "I know what I'm going to do here. I'm going to bridge these hills with graceful arches." There were multiple hills. And he saw multiple bridging and multiple arches, which were a reflection of those hills.

In the ensuing months, Green with Summers interviewed, researched, and sized up the complex functional needs of the various departments that would use the center. Months later, Wright prepared his first schematic at Taliesin, using that functional information. The sketch was his first commitment of the center's spatial order to paper and was not unlike Wright's earlier vision of Broadacre's civic buildings. Wright designed a civic center in which the bulk of the county's offices were placed in a long building bridging the ravines between three adjacent hills (Figure 6-10), with a huge fairground tent and lagoon nearby. Inside the main building, offices were placed on either side of a multiple-storied interior street in which citizens, lobbyists, politicians, bureaucrats, judges, police, and children rubbed shoulders (Figure 6-11). This street was not to be a localite, austere, and impressive public front or a localite back corridor serving clandestine political meetings. The interior street opened up government. It ran the full length of the building, absorbing incoming pedestrian and vehicular traffic below, spilling out onto terraces on the tops of the hills and opening to the sky above (Figure 6-11).

FIGURE 6–10. Frank Lloyd Wright:
Marin County Civic Center, San
Rafael, California

Photo: Glenn Lym

At the center of the building, Wright topped the middle hill with the county library under a large dome (Figure 6-10). The supervisors' chambers were on the floor below. This was a deliberate act to articulate more thoroughly his spatial order of the center as a bridge that the citizens of Marin would like coming to and by which government would be ventilated and oriented toward its people. Green talked about that library.

The Librarian did not like the idea of having her library in part of that building. She would have wanted her separate little domain. Frank Lloyd Wright felt that that was the best place for children to be exposed to government, and it would help educate the politicians. The employees could make use of it during their off lunch periods. It would be good for the whole community.

And Summers elaborated on this.

I saw this dome and expected it would be the seat of government, to be the Board of Supervisors. I was astonished that it was the library. The supervisors private offices are thus [below on] the ground whereas the library is [above in] a place of seclusion. At this time Wright told me that he was now working with the circle as something which was in itself a concept of completeness . . . [Here was] learning as completeness above the actual process of government below.

Wright presented his design at a public meeting in which he answered questions as he and his audience moved from drawing to drawing in a high school cafeteria. The drawings then went on display throughout the county. In February 1960, construction began on phase one.

FIGURE 6–11. Frank Lloyd Wright: Marin County Civic Center

Photo: Glenn Lym

In 1960, events shaped up that would cast doubt on the center's completion. Wright had died a year earlier, at the age of 89. Green and Taliesin Fellowship continued the work. But in Marin, the reformers were under sharp attack, and 1960 was an election year. The county budget now required new tax increases. The county needed a new hospital and juvenile hall, which meant again new taxes. The localites went into the election having a reputation of opposing the reformers' spending. Schultz and another reformer lost their bids for reelection. By 1961, the localites were in power. They ordered construction on the civic center stopped immediately. The localite board said it wanted to see if the new building could be converted into a hospital. A public outrage followed. Polls found that, although the citizens had voted the reformers out of power, those citizens nonetheless were committed to their new civic center eighteen to one. Consultants reported to the board that remodeling the new center into a hospital was not practical. The localite board voted to remove its stop-work order, but moved on to abolish the office of the county administrator, returning those powers to county departments and supervisors. This precipitated another outcry and a recall movement that resulted in the replacement of a localite by a reformer on the board. By 1962, the reformers were back in power and quickly moved to reestablish their vision of government. They reestablished the office of the county administrator and moved to assure completion of the later phases of the civic center according to Wright's plans.

STRATEGIC WORK. Wright was a master of strategic work. He correctly understood the important social-spatial issues at stake. He understood that they would be decided by the voters. So Wright campaigned, first before the board of supervisors and then before the public. His approach was direct and incisive. He dealt with his reformist clients, his users, and his detractors directly on the basis of spatial orders, pointing to the relationship of space and social values. He sought out and listened to reformist and departmental heads' spatial orders for the center. He reshaped those spatial orders into a spatial order of Marin County and its civic center. Later, because they felt their own spatial orders for the county and the center were being realized, the voters supported the center's construction despite their fiscally conservative mood.

STRATEGIC VISION.   The Marin County reformers had a clear social vision in mind when they sought an architect. In Wright, they found a designer who understood and expanded upon that vision. Wright had anticipated Marin's problems some twenty years earlier in his Broadacre City schemes. So he came to Marin with a pre-made spatial order for the county's growth.

In his work on the center proper, he built upon the reformers' spatial order of a nonimposing, friendly place for citizens and civil servants alike. He saw the highway street as a means for freeing people to live dispersed and close to the land. Yet, the street would bring them to the civic center and penetrate its building, creating an inviting, friendly civic place. Inside, a pedestrian street opened up government to its citizens. Sunlight, breezes, children, politicians, cars, and trees mixed in the corridors of the civic center, creating a new space for reformist government.

Wright and his clients had suppressed the localite spatial order of a government of private interests and domains. Yet, the center's pedestrian street provided for departmental work domains in a way never achieved at ATT. County work domains were free to grow or shrink behind the interior corridor's movable glass and aluminum walls. At Marin, there was to be spatial freedom for departmental in-fighting and expansion as well as for citizens, politicians, and sunlight.

strategic vision

In a design process, designer and user spatial orders must be addressed with strategic vision, which can come in two different ways. Strategic vision may come from the design process itself. Here, the net intelligence and sensitivity of all its participants display strategic vision in seeking out, excluding, and synthesizing the design as at Kresge College. Or strategic vision may also come from a critical participant as with Frank Lloyd Wright at Marin.

Whether by collective or individual will, a design process with strategic vision is characterized ideally by three properties. One, a full range of important and possibly conflicting spatial orders is *uncovered* in the process of designing. Strategic work is undertaken to locate latent user expectations. One way or another, the design process creates the space for clients and users to venture their "it's unimportant but it's on the tip of my tongue" type remarks that are keys to hidden spatial orders. The design process seeks a disclosure of the full range of spatial orders bearing upon the project at hand.

Two, a design process with strategic vision *sees* that full range of spatial orders. Trivia and conflicts are not suppressed but are put into a context. Designer and user decision makers are emotionally willing to embrace discrepant, irritating, and conflicting spatial orders. They see the thrust of these spatial orders.

Three, in a design process with strategic vision, a design spatial order emerges that embodies a *vision* of the institution. The basis of inclusion or exclusion of spatial orders into the design spatial order lies in seeking the singular truth that underlies the range of the institution's spatial orders. It is not based upon ignorance nor irritations.

Thus, a design process with strategic vision accepts the people and institution being designed for. It incisively sees their renewal as an outcome of design. As in Kresge College or in the Marin County Civic Center, design processes with strategic vision result in built-environments sensitive to hidden as well as obvious institutional issues. At Kresge, the design process eventually attended to the contradictory issues of a community as an organic order deriving from its parts and as an overall civic order somewhat removed from the order of its individual parts. At Marin, the design process immediately dealt with the localites' emphasis on a "back room" government and the reformers' emphasis on a centralized, open government. Kresge College and Marin County were opened up to themselves by facing legitimate yet latent institutional issues during their design processes.

In contrast, design processes without strategic vision suppress or overlook important spatial orders. Here the design process is neurotic. It does not attain a full vision of its institution. The design fixates people as they continually circle around unattended, unseen, and unaccepted institutional issues. At ATT, the design process failed to address the conflict of overall order versus the order of individual work domains. The ATT design process suppressed and ignored the latter. In not coming to terms with spatial order conflicts, no design vision emerged to open that institution to itself and its future.

At the beginning of this book, we talked of our romance with space. In discussing acute and chronic space experience, we were essentially pointing out the unity in our experience of, reflection on, and impulses to shape space. In these experiences in which our lives fold into space, our thoughts about ourselves, our worlds, and space are one. More complex and long-term efforts to shape and design space lose this spontaneous unity between space and social vision. So strategic vision is necessary to restore this unity to complex design processes. Strategic vision cuts through the maze of spatial orders impinging on a design process to see the heart of an institution. In this way, there can be a connection between the intelligence shaping the institution and the intelligence shaping the space of that institution. A design process with strategic vision enables an institution to envision itself and space simultaneously and, thus, to fulfill its own basic romance with space.

index

Abstraction, 22–25
Acute space, 2–6, 9, 13
   social situation rules and,
      18–20, 22–25
   symbol formation in,
      25–27
American Indians, 6–7
Apartments:
   low-income housing
      complexes, 50–51
   in reference
      communities, 51–54
   social situation rules and,
      20–22, *22*
   spatial order in, 40–47,
      41, 43, 45, 47
Arnheim, Rudolf, 24
ATT offices, San Francisco,
   116–24, *118, 119, 120,*
   122, 123, 148

Bettelheim, Bruno, 18
Black Elk, 6
Bollingen House, *36,*
   36–38, *37, 38, 39,* 40,
   49
Boorstin, Daniel, 52
Briones Park, California, *19*
Broadcare City, 76–77, 140
Bruner, Jerome, 23

Campbell, D. T., 16
Carpentered world, 16–17,
   17
Chronic space, 8–13, 81
   professional designers
      and, 81
   social situation rules and,
      20–25
   symbol formation in,
      27–29

Church Street South
   Housing, New Haven,
   Connecticut, *50,*
   50–51
Conflicting spatial orders,
   112–13
Consumption community,
   52
Convent of Saint Mary of La
   Tourette, Eveux,
   France, 70–72, *71*

Dark wood fortress project,
   101–6, *104, 105*
Design concept, 70 (see
   also Spatial orders)
Douglas, Mary, 9

Edgar, Robert, 127–28,
   130, 131, 136–37
Eisenman, Peter, 65–66,
   66, 67, 81–82, *83*
Eliade, Mircea, 7–8
External order of homes,
   32, 48–54

Fit theory, 96–97
Francis, Earl L., 49
Freud, Sigmund, 9, 23,
   32–33
Fried, Mark, 49–50
Fusselman, N., 138–42

Goldstein, Kurt, 22–23
Green, Aaron, 139, 140,
   143, 144, 146
Gropius, Walter, 2

Head-body office, 12, *12*
Herskovits, M. J., 16
Heurtley House, Oak Park,
    Illinois, *56*
Homes:
    spatial order of, 31–61
        external, 32, 48–54; *of
        Frank Lloyd Wright,*
        54–55, *55, 56, 57,
        57*–59, *59*, 73–76, *74,
        75*; *internal*, 32–48
    strategic vision and:
        *dark wood fortress
        project*, 101–6, *104,
        105*; *kitchen project*,
        97–101, *99*; *small
        house project*, 106–9,
        108, 110, 111
House III, 65–66, *66, 67*,
    81–82, *83*
Humane world-functional
    world apartment,
    10–11, *11*

Imagery, thinking by,
    22–25
Improvisational spaces, 18
Institute of Management,
    Ahmedabad, India,
    77–78, *79*
Institutions, large, 116–47
    ATT offices, 116–24, *118,
    119, 120, 122, 123,*
    148
    Kresge College, 124–28,
    126, 129, 130, 130–37,
    134, 148
    Marin County Civic
    Center, 137–48, *144,
    145*
Intelligence of space, 13
Internal order of homes,
    32–48

Japanese tea ceremony, 7
John Deere Building,
    Moline, Illinois, 68–70,
    69
Jung, Carl, 25–26, *26, 36,
    36*–38, *37, 38, 39*, 40

Kahn, Louis I., 77–81, *79,
    80*, 82–93, *85, 86, 87,
    88*
Kant, Immanuel, 24
Kitchen project, 97–101, *99*
Kresge College, 124–28,
    126, 129, 130, 130–37,
    134, 148

Laguna, Grace de, 16
Le Corbusier, 70–72, *71*, 81
Lee, Terence, 66, 68
Lew, Eugene, and
    Associates, 116–24,
    *118, 119, 120, 122,
    123*
Low-income housing
    complexes, 50–51

Marin County Civic Center,
    137–48, *144, 145*
Marlin, Bill, 84
Moore, Charles, 50,
    125–28, *126, 129, 130*,
    131–33, *134*, 137
Müller-Lyre illusion, 17, *17*

Neutra, Richard, 142
Neutral space, 2, 16

Pei, I. M., 64
Personal expression of
    architects, 64–68

Phillips Exeter Academy Library, New Hampshire, 82–93, *85, 86, 87, 88, 90, 91*
Political interests in design, 96–97
Prairie Houses, 54, 56, 58, 59, *59,* 73–75, *74*
Primary objects, 16
Profane space, 7–8
Professional building, 64–93
  personal expression, 64–68
  professionals' vs. users' spatial orders, 81–93
  spatial orders of professional designers, 68–81
Pueblo Indians, 6

Rauch, Venturi and, *65*
Reference community, 51–54
Ritual, 9–12

Saarinen, Eero, 68–70, *69*
Sacred space, 7–8
Scheerer, Martin, 22–23
Schmidt, Clarence, 34–35, 48–49
Schmidt House, Woodstock, New York, 34–35, *35,* 40
Schultz, Vera, 138, 140, 146
Scully, Vincent, 6
Secondary objects, 16
Segall, M. H., 16
Small house project, 106–9, *108, 110,* 111
Smith, Norris Kelly, 55

Social situation rules, 18–25
Somner, Robert, 66–67, 68
Space:
  acute, 2–6, 9, 13
    social situation rules and, 18–20, 22–25; *symbol formation in,* 25–27
  chronic, 8–13, 81
    professional designers and, 81; *social situation rules and,* 20–25; *symbol formation in,* 27–29
  intelligence of, 13
  neutral, 2, 16
  profane, 7–8
  sacred, 7–8
  western denial of relationship with, 6–8
  (*see also* Spatial orders)
Spatial orders:
  of homes, 31–61
    external, 32, 48–54; *of Frank Lloyd Wright,* 54–55, *55, 56, 57,* 57–59, *59,* 73–76, *74, 75; internal,* 32–48
  learning and thinking with space, 16–25
  in professional building, 64–93
    personal expression and, 64–68; *professional designers,* 68–81; *professionals' vs. users',* 81–93
  strategic vision and (*see* Strategic vision)
  symbol formation and, 25–29
Strategic vision, 96–149
  characterization of, 147–49

Strategic vision (*cont.*)
  design projects:
    *conflicting spatial
    orders and,* 112–13;
    dark wood fortress,
    101–6, *104, 105;*
    kitchen, 97–101, *99;*
    small house, 106–9,
    108, 110, 111
  large institutions and,
    116–47
    ATT offices, 116–24,
    *118, 119, 120, 122,
    123,* 148; *Kresge
    College,* 124–28, *126,
    129, 130,* 130–37, *134,*
    148; *Marin County
    Civic Center,* 137–48,
    144, 145
  political interests in
    design, 96–97
Strategic work, 97, 101,
    111, 124, 146
Structured spaces, 18
Subliminal rules, 18–25
Summers, Mary, 139–40,
    142–45
Symbol formation, 25–29

Taliesin I, Spring Green,
    Wisconsin, 58–59, *59*
Taliesin II, Spring Green,
    Wisconsin, 59
Theater of Performing Arts,
    Fort Wayne, Indiana,
    78–80, *80*

Tomek, F. F., House,
    Riverside, Illinois, *74,*
    74–75
Turnbull William, 50,
    125–28, 126, *129, 130,*
    130–37, *134*

Unity Church, Oak Park,
    Illinois, 72–73, *73*
Users' spatial orders, vs.
    professionals' spatial
    orders, 81–93 (*see
    also* Strategic vision)
Usonian House, *75,* 75–76

Venturi, Robert, 64–65, *65*

West End (Boston
    community), 49–50
Wright, Frank Lloyd, 54–55,
    55, 56, 57, 57–59, *59,*
    64, 72–77, *73, 74, 75,*
    81, 137–147, *144, 145*

Y.M.C.A., Canton, Ohio,
    64–65, *65*